SO-AGY-189

Especially For

....

From

....

Date

....

FROM
GOD'S WORD
TO A
WOMAN'S HEART

A DEVOTIONAL

JANICE THOMPSON

BARBOUR BOOKS
An Imprint of Barbour Publishing, Inc.

© 2014 by Barbour Publishing, Inc.

ISBN 978-1-64352-280-7

eBook Editions:
Adobe Digital Edition (.epub) 978-1-63058-546-4
Kindle and MobiPocket Edition (.prc) 978-1-63058-547-1

All rights reserved. No part of this publication may be reproduced or transmitted for commercial purposes, except for brief quotations in printed reviews, without written permission of the publisher.

Churches and other noncommercial interests may reproduce portions of this book without the express written permission of Barbour Publishing, provided that the text does not exceed 500 words or 5 percent of the entire book, whichever is less, and that the text is not material quoted from another publisher. When reproducing text from this book, include the following credit line: "From *From God's Word to a Woman's Heart*, published by Barbour Publishing, Inc. Used by permission."

Scripture quotations marked KJV are taken from the King James Version of the Bible.

Scripture quotations marked NKJV are taken from the New King James Version®. Copyright © 1982 by Thomas Nelson, Inc. Used by permission. All rights reserved.

Scripture quotations marked NLT are taken from the *Holy Bible*. New Living Translation copyright© 1996, 2004, 2015 by Tyndale House Foundation. Used by permission of Tyndale House Publishers, Inc. Carol Stream, Illinois 60188. All rights reserved.

Scripture quotations marked NIV are taken from the HOLY BIBLE, NEW INTERNATIONAL VERSION®. NIV®. Copyright © 1973, 1978, 1984, 2011 by Biblica, Inc.™ Used by permission. All rights reserved worldwide.

Scripture quotations marked GW are taken from GOD'S WORD®, © 1995 God's Word to the Nations. Used by permission of Baker Publishing Group.

Scripture quotations marked CEV are from the Contemporary English Version, Copyright © 1995 by American Bible Society. Used by permission.

Scripture quotations marked ESV are from The Holy Bible, English Standard Version®, copyright © 2001 by Crossway Bibles, a publishing ministry of Good News Publishers. Used by permission. All rights reserved.

Scripture quotations marked NASB are taken from the New American Standard Bible, © 1960, 1962, 1963, 1968, 1971, 1972, 1973, 1975, 1977, 1995 by The Lockman Foundation. Used by permission.

Published by Barbour Books, an imprint of Barbour Publishing, Inc., 1810 Barbour Drive, Uhrichsville, Ohio 44683, www.barbourbooks.com

Our mission is to inspire the world with the life-changing message of the Bible.

Member of the
Evangelical Christian
Publishers Association

Printed in China.

INTRODUCTION

Women of God are women of purpose. They have the innate sense that they were put on planet earth to accomplish something great for the kingdom of God. Having a sense of purpose will drive you. Think of it as the proverbial fuel in your car. You wouldn't get very far without it.

Perhaps you're struggling. You can't seem to find your purpose in life. This inspiring collection will be perfect for you. In reading through these devotions, you will discover a sense of adventure and courage that will motivate you to ask the questions: "Lord, why did You create me?" and "What is Your will/desire for me today, Father?"

Of course, no one—male or female—can discover their sense of purpose until they enter a relationship with their Creator. Knowing Him, hearing His heartbeat, figuring out His plans for your life. . . these are all dependent on walking with your hand in His. So, let's start there. Have you taken that first step toward God? Have you surrendered your heart, your life to Him? If not, take hold of His hand today. Let Him sweep you into a relationship unlike any other you've ever experienced. Then hang on for the ride as He reveals plan after plan, adventure after adventure.

Are you ready, woman of purpose? It's all eyes forward from this point on. No looking over your shoulder. No "I live such a humdrum life." Toss those words and replace them with, "Where are we going today, Lord?" and "I wonder what amazing things God has planned for me around that next bend."

Your best days are ahead, so what's holding you back? Ready, set. . .go!

YOU ARE LOVED

In this the love of God was made manifest among us, that God sent his only Son into the world, so that we might live through him. In this is love, not that we have loved God but that he loved us and sent his Son to be the propitiation for our sins. Beloved, if God so loved us, we also ought to love one another. No one has ever seen God; if we love one another, God abides in us and his love is perfected in us.

1 JOHN 4:9–12 ESV

You can't drum up a sense of purpose. You can strategize, plan, set goals. . .but even the most talented, driven woman can't create a true, internal "sense" of purpose. She can put on her broadest smile, speak in her most cheerful voice, but if she's wilting on the inside, then what she's portraying on the outside is just a facade. And let's face it. . .no one likes a phony, especially not the one doing the pretending. And there's only so long you can keep it up, anyway. That whole "fake it till you make it" thing doesn't work when it comes to feeling a true, internal sense of fulfillment.

So, let's talk about how to "get" purpose. If you can't strategize, plan, or design your own life purpose, where do you get it? Only one place—your heavenly Father. He longs for you to know why you were created, and loves it when you catch the vision of how big, how consequential, how exciting your life can be. And all of this comes as a

result of one word: *love*.

When you come to grips with God's overwhelming love for you, when you realize the depth of His passion for you as His daughter, you can't help but be overcome with gratitude. And gratitude is a great motivator. It lifts you up and sets your feet in a higher place. It propels you to accomplish things that you never accomplished before. It gives you courage that the Cowardly Lion would be tickled to have.

Knowing you are loved—deeply, intimately loved—just does something to you, doesn't it? We're all searching for that type of love, and when we find it through the person of Jesus Christ, we're blown away. But, why does God love you like He does? Because you're His child. And, as His child, He desires a sweet, "Climb in my lap and let's talk about your day" relationship. Having that kind of intimacy with the One who created you, the One who knows you best, gives you a sense of purpose unlike any other. Love propels. Love motivates. Love sends you off on a journey filled with delight and joy.

Today, pause for a moment and thank God for His deep, abiding love for you. When you surrender yourself to that love, you open yourself up to a road filled with excitement. No more "humdrumness" for you, sweet sister. You've got a lot to accomplish—with His strength and His name. So, what's keeping you? Get out there and make a difference in your world, and may love—His love—lead the way.

YOU ARE UNIQUE

But you are a chosen people, a royal priesthood,
a holy nation, God's special possession, that you may
declare the praises of him who called you out
of darkness into his wonderful light.

1 PETER 2:9 NIV

You are unique. There's no one like you on planet earth. Sure, others might have your hair color, your skin tone, or your Southern drawl, but there's no one just like you. It's not just your unique fingerprint that sets you apart. Your heart, your love for others. . .it's all an intricate part of God's clever and creative design when He came up with the idea of breathing life into you.

Maybe you're like Catherine, a teen girl who felt she was a little *too* unique, too different. The youngest of three sisters, she felt like the odd man out. Her talents and abilities were different from her older sisters. Her figure was different. Her curves were a little curvier. Even her personality was different. Her older sisters had gregarious, outgoing temperaments. She tended to be more withdrawn and shy. Catherine's parents did their best to encourage her, but it did little good. Instead of celebrating her uniqueness, she fought it at every turn. Only when she reached adulthood did Catherine begin to see her differences as an asset, not a detriment.

Maybe you can relate. Maybe you see your uniqueness—those

little things that set you apart from other women, both physically and psychologically—as a problem. You don't look in the mirror and say, "Wow, look how special I am because I'm different." Maybe you say, "Ugh! Why can't I look like everyone else?"

How do you overcome these feelings? By coming to grips with the fact that uniqueness isn't a curse; it's a blessing. Think about it. God never intended for His girls to be cookie cutters. (How boring would that be, anyway?) We each have our own individual style and persona. Picture the Almighty putting a little stamp on your forehead that reads, "Unique! Individually designed! This one's different. . .and I like it!" On the other hand, if God stamped your forehead, He'd have to stamp everyone else's too, because we're all uniquely created. Just like snowflakes, no two women are alike, nor should they strive to be.

Don't reshape yourself to look, act, be like everyone else. Don't fret your differences. Instead, make up your mind to celebrate them! Understanding and appreciating your uniqueness is incredibly freeing. When you're happy to be a one-of-a-kind, each little "difference" is a special trait. "There's only one me!" becomes a motto you can be proud of. So what are you waiting for? Celebrate your one-of-a-kind design and watch as God frees you to accomplish great things that only you can accomplish!

YOU CAN ACCOMPLISH MANY GOALS

"But you, take courage! Do not let your hands
be weak, for your work shall be rewarded."
2 CHRONICLES 15:7 ESV

It's tough to accomplish goals if you don't set them. That's why it's so important to look to the road ahead with hope and excitement, to strategize, to dream. We're not supposed to worry about the future, but we are encouraged to plan for it.

Consider the story of Jeannie. She longed to start her own interior decorating company. She dreamed about it for years, in fact, but she rarely acted on it. Sure, she wanted to step out in faith, but life always seemed to get in the way. She didn't create a workable plan for her company, so the business never got off the ground. Though she never spoke about it publicly, this ate at her on the inside. Every time Jeannie came across a successful businesswoman (a friend, a family member, or someone in her church), she struggled with jealousy. "Why is she doing so well with her business, and I'm not?"

The answer, of course, could be found in this statement: "To be successful, you must strategize." Instead of putting together a plan, Jeannie just shrugged, swallowed down her bitterness, and went back to her everyday life. She tucked away her ambition, afraid she couldn't accomplish her goals. And, truth be told, she couldn't accomplish them. . . because she gave up too quickly.

So, how do you feel about strategy, woman of purpose? Are you a goal setter? Are you a strategizer? The Lord wants to be the center of your plans, and He gets excited when you trust Him for things that seem bigger than you are. So, why not close your eyes and ponder the "what ifs." What dream have you let go of because it seemed impossible? Maybe it's time to ask the Lord if He wants to resurrect that dream. Then, with His help, put together a plan of action.

What sort of action, you ask? Lay down a workable schedule. Create a spreadsheet that you can refer to daily, one that implements a solid plan of action, step by step. If you're longing to write a book, set aside writing time. If you want to create an interior design company, make sure you put together a step-by-step plan, one that incorporates both the business side and the design side. Then step out of your comfort zone and—step by step—do the things on your list. You might be inching your way toward the goal, but at least you're making progress.

The point is, you have to set goals or you'll surely never reach them. What are you waiting for, woman of purpose? Open that spreadsheet file and start jotting down some goals! You might be surprised to see where the road takes you!

YOU'VE SETTLED THE "FOREVER" ISSUE

For God so loved the world that he gave his
one and only Son, that whoever believes in
him shall not perish but have eternal life.

JOHN 3:16 NIV

Many women have not recognized their purpose because they simply haven't figured out the true meaning of life in Christ. Once you give your heart to Him, purpose swells up inside of you like yeast in a mound of yet-uncooked bread. When you walk in ongoing relationship with your Creator, you begin to see this life—your time on earth—as just a foretaste of the life to come in heaven. It's all one continuous journey.

Pause to think about that. Most of us are so fascinated by what's happening right in front of us. We don't have an eternal perspective. We're dealing with paying the mortgage, taking the kids to the pediatrician, driving back and forth to soccer practice, Bible study at church, the grocery store. We forget that the "stuff" happening right in front of us is just a teensy-tiny glimpse of the "forever" story.

Have you settled the forever issue? If not, then take a look at the first four books of the New Testament and read about the life of Jesus. He humbled Himself by coming to this earth, not for His own purposes, but for you. That's right. . .you! He came as an advocate—a middleman—to carry the weight of your sins, your mistakes. He carried those sins all the way to the cross, where His blood spilled out as a sacrifice for all of

humankind. He never sinned, and yet He died for the sins of humankind, so that we could all have the opportunity to live. . .forever! No longer would our sin separate us from God!

What does He ask in return? Your heart. Your love. Your dedication. And here's a little secret: Once you fall in love with Him, once you offer your heart in adoration to the One who carried your sins, you are happy to serve Him with your life. You can't wait to spend intimate time with Him, asking questions like, "Lord, how can I be usable to You today?" or "Father, how can I reach out to those around me and show them Your love today?"

The point is, you will have a radical sense of purpose when you understand God's love for you. And that purpose won't just be about today. Or tomorrow. Or the next day. Your purpose will extend to include all of eternity. You will look at your next door neighbor and think, "How can I reach her so that she can share in eternity with me?" You will no longer flinch at that rude salesman who comes to your door. Instead, you will wonder how you can minister to him, to let him know about God's love.

Your purpose will grow as your "eternal" perspective grows. And what a wonderful perspective it is!

The Lord will fulfill his purpose for me;
your steadfast love, O LORD, endures forever.
Do not forsake the work of your hands.

PSALM 138:8 ESV

To have purpose means you have a reason. Think about that for a moment. If you have a new puppy, you have a reason to take walks in the sunshine. If you have a job, you have a reason to get out of bed in the morning. If you have children who need to be fed, you have a reason for cooking. Though "purpose" can't be seen with your eyes, it's your defining "reason" for doing what you do. It propels. It motivates. It drives.

You have purpose. Pause to think through the meaning in those words in light of what we've already discussed. You have a significant reason for being on planet earth. You weren't placed here by accident. On the contrary! You are a difference maker. A life changer. A "we can't do without her, wouldn't even want to try!" gal. Your eternal purpose harkens back to the call that God placed on your life before you were even born.

Take a second to think about that. God placed His desires inside of you before you ever breathed your first breath. Your unique, creative design was on His heart before you made your entrance into the world. He had a plan for your life and hoped you would catch the vision.

Have you? Have you caught the vision for all that you can accomplish for Him? Maybe you're ready to roll, anxious to get busy. You've discovered your unique giftings and, as a result, have put together a plan. Your heart is beating. Your imagination is in overdrive. You're more than ready, because you know there's work to be done. Don't hold back, sister! Step out of your comfort zone and give in to your life purpose! No, you can't see it with your eyes, but you can sense it in your heart.

Consider the story of Belinda. She felt an inner prompting from the time she was young, one that wouldn't leave her alone. It motivated her to draw close to the Lord. It nudged her to go to Bible college. It motivated her to marry a godly man who had similar ideals. It drove her to start a Christian school of the arts for boys and girls so they could discover their unique giftings. It carried on as she poured into life after life, child after child, adult after adult. And it all went back to a "feeling" she had as a child that she was put on this planet to do something special, something significant, because of her great love for her heavenly Father. Talk about exciting!

Do you feel Belinda's passion for life? Do you share a similar zeal? Are you prompted daily by that "I have to get going" feeling? If so, rejoice! These things are heavenly gifts, straight from the Father's heart to yours. So don't wait any longer. Dive right in to your life purpose!

YOUR BODY IS A VESSEL

Or do you not know that your body is a temple
of the Holy Spirit within you, whom you have from God?
You are not your own, for you were bought with
a price. So glorify God in your body.

1 CORINTHIANS 6:19–20 ESV

Some women seem to have more drive, more initiative than others. They sense their unique calling and are always ready to respond. Many of the rest of us are tired. We're "wrung out" (as Great-Grandma might've said) because we're overworked and overcommitted. A woman of purpose has to have the energy to do the things she's called by God to do, and that starts with taking care of her body. When your body is exhausted, you're not going to be able to function the same.

Your body is a vessel. A temple. The Spirit of God resides inside of that temple. And it's critical that you keep that temple in good shape, not just for your own good, but for the sake of those around you and for the sake of the Gospel. You're preaching a sermon with your life, after all. And if the message is always the same: "Overworked! Worn out! Poor eating habits!" then perhaps others won't be as interested in what you're promoting.

Maybe it's time for a change. A change in sleeping habits. Change in diet. Change in exercise. Perhaps it's even time for a change in perspective. Maybe you need to look at your life, your situation, in a

new and different way. If so, you will appreciate Marcia's story. She gave of her time, her talents, her energies in a thousand ways, never saying no to anyone or anything. As a motivated, driven woman, the word no simply wasn't in her vocabulary.

Until she got sick. Her body began to rebel, and she found herself in bed for several days in a row, unable to function. It took some one-on-one time with the Lord and a great deal of mental anguish before she finally came to grips with the fact that the very thing that drove her—motivation, zeal—would be her undoing if she didn't take care of herself.

And so, she changed gears. Still driven. Still motivated. But now, balanced. She made up her mind to only say yes to the things that had God's stamp of approval. Sure, she hurt a few feelings by bowing out of things, but ultimately her health mattered more than pleasing people.

Can you relate to Marcia's tale? If so, maybe it's time to reanalyze your yeses and offer a few nos. You've only got one body and need to take the best possible care of it. Balance is key, woman of purpose!

YOU CAN TUNE OUT NEGATIVITY

In your relationships with one another, have the same
mindset as Christ Jesus: Who, being in very nature God,
did not consider equality with God something to be
used to his own advantage; rather, he made himself
nothing by taking the very nature of a servant,
being made in human likeness.

PHILIPPIANS 2:5–7 NIV

Aren't you glad to know you can tune out the negative voices around you? Sure, they're everywhere—at home, in the workplace, on the television. But the naysayers won't get you down when your thoughts are focused on what the Word of God says about you.

So what if the negative voices at work or at your school say you're a failure? Who cares if your parents didn't think you would make anything of your life? Why fret over the teachers who said you'd never amount to anything? God's Word says that you are a champion, a difference maker. What does it matter if negative voices in your head tell you you'll never measure up to the other women at your church or in your neighborhood? The Bible says that you have all you need in Christ. And why get distressed if you try something and fail? Failing is a great motivator to try again, isn't it?

Sure, there will always be those who think they're better than you are—and let's face it, there will always be people who can cook better,

look better, or present a better picture of the ideal life—but God says that you are complete and lacking nothing. Your focus should remain on the Lord, not on people, especially those bent on bringing you down.

So muffle the voices around you by memorizing scripture verses. Display carefully chosen ones on your walls. Put motivational verses on your bathroom mirror, your refrigerator, or your car's dashboard. Put them every place you go so that you never forget what the Lord thinks—and says—about you. Before long, they will be a natural part of your conversation and your thoughts. The words you've memorized will be your first response to the negative voices around you. Talk about encouraging!

Whenever you feel defeated, speak the Word of God aloud. Sing songs of praise. Before long you won't remember the ugly words that were spoken over you. The "you won't make it" or "who do you think you are to try something like that?" will be muffled by the joy in your heart. You will only remember what God says about you. And what He says. . . well, it's all good! Chew on that awhile, woman of purpose. Before long you'll feel motivated to try, and try again. And those negative voices around you? Why, you won't even hear them. You'll be so busy singing praises to your heavenly Father that you'll drown them out.

YOU HAVE AN ATTITUDE OF GRATITUDE

Let the message of Christ dwell among you richly
as you teach and admonish one another with all
wisdom through psalms, hymns, and songs from the
Spirit, singing to God with gratitude in your hearts.

COLOSSIANS 3:16 NIV

Women of purpose see the bigger picture. They're not focused on self or on the various things that go wrong in day-to-day living. They see each moment, each sunrise, each smile from a child or nuzzle of a puppy's nose as a gift. They've learned the secret: gratitude isn't something we have to conjure up. When you're head over heels in love with the God who created you, it's easy to be grateful.

Motivational speaker and teacher Zig Ziglar coined the phrase "Have an attitude of gratitude," and he was right! This attitude (which is the same attitude that was in Christ Jesus) helps so much. When you're grateful for every little thing, guess what? You discover even more to be grateful for. The "little" blessings become big to you. You have a genuine thankfulness in your heart for life's many joys.

Regina understood this, for sure. She was raised in a home where gratitude was a natural part of life, where her parents paused in the middle of a situation or circumstance to offer up praise to God for every little blessing. It became a part of her nature to see the good in things, to see the glass as half full. Others wondered if she was "for

real" because of her positive, upbeat, bubbly personality. She was! You could pinch her, poke her, knock her down. . .and she would still find a way to bless God in the middle of it. And she wasn't faking it, either! How could she live like this? She had an innate attitude of gratitude, and it saw her through both good times and bad.

Gratitude. Thankfulness. Appreciation. The very words that drove Regina to live her life in such a way are words that most of us rarely pause to think through. We should. When you're a woman of purpose, when you understand God's unique stamp and call on your life, then you realize just how important it is to be grateful for the things He's doing in your life, great and small! It's been said that you can have a "trait" of gratitude or a "state" of gratitude. It's up to you to decide which one!

So what are you grateful for today? If you're like Regina, you face good and bad circumstances. Choose to respond to all of them with an attitude of gratefulness in your heart, then watch as God gives you even more to be thankful for!

YOU'VE BEEN RENEWED

Therefore we do not lose heart. Though outwardly we are
wasting away, yet inwardly we are being renewed day by day.
2 Corinthians 4:16 niv

Have you ever pondered the word "renewed?" The prefix "re-" means
"again." So, to be renewed is to be made new. . .again. The word conjures
images of fresh starts. New days dawning. Past things being put in their
proper place. . .in the past!

Why is this important to you as a woman of purpose? Because, sweet
sister, you (like all of the great women before you) will feel like giving
up at times. You will wish for a new situation, a new perspective, a new
opportunity, a new chance. You will need a new vision, a new sense of
hope, a new perspective. And you can have it. You can be renewed in
a way that will change your life forever.

Consider the story of Jane. She lived most of her adult life in a rough
marriage. After many years, the relationship came to an abrupt end. Jane
was devastated. She didn't want to go backward but couldn't figure out
how to move forward, either. What she needed—and eventually got—was
a new perspective. She asked the Lord to renew her vision, to give her
new hope, new dreams. She placed her life in His hands, and God, the
Almighty Author of her story, began a work inside her that included
many "new" things: a new job, a new place to live, a new outlook. Sure,
she still struggled with some past issues, but with her hope renewed,

she didn't find herself glancing over her shoulder as much as she once had. Best of all, she had a renewed sense of hope, which brought energy and vitality to her life once again.

What about you? Are there some areas of your life that need to be renewed? Does your hope need to be restored? Do you need a reason to put one foot in front of the other? Perhaps your story is different from Jane's, but the overarching issue is the same: you need a fresh start. No matter what you're facing, your perspective, your outlook can be made new again. God is in the restoration business. Nothing is too difficult for Him. He can take the old, breathe life into it, and give you hope for the future, far above what you dared believe possible.

Trust Him today, woman of purpose. Reignite your passion for Him, and then watch as He renews your vision, your perspective, and your hope.

YOU ARE NOT AFRAID OF CHANGE

Therefore, if anyone is in Christ, the new creation
has come: The old has gone, the new is here!

2 CORINTHIANS 5:17 NIV

Some people cringe at the idea of change. New job. New house. New relationship. Shifting from one church to another. The empty nest years. So many times in life we have to begin again. It's inevitable, and we have to face it, but it's rarely fun. In fact, our stress level can go up—way up—when we face change.

Perhaps the word "again" is the real enemy here. To begin "again" makes us feel as if something went wrong the last time. But that's not always the case. Sometimes we just have to get to a new place, even when the "old" one seemed perfectly fine. Sure, it's hard, but you can do it, with God's help.

Maybe you feel stuck. Your feet are in the mud. Starting over conjures up images of exhaustion. Feels like too much work. And talk about risk! Who needs that kind of stress? Still, you wish things could change. Maybe you're in a job—or a relationship—that you want out of, but you don't know how to take that first step. The idea of change feels daunting. You're scared. What's a woman to do?

Consider Cheryl's story: She and her husband raised their four daughters in the same house her parents had lived in. Cheryl loved that home. It was familiar. Comfortable. Everything about it rang true. Then,

just as her youngest daughter left the nest, she was forced to move to a new place. The circumstances were beyond her control and she felt completely lost. Starting over. . .at this stage of life? Thankfully, she settled in well in the new place and went on to make many wonderful memories with her children (and eventually grandchildren) in her new house. But getting there was tough!

Here's something to ponder today: The word *risk* isn't a bad word. Whenever you face the fear of the unknown, it can feel risky, but isn't that where faith comes in? All of life is a risk. Each venture, every challenge, each "blind faith move" involves stepping out into the vast unknown and trusting that God—who adores you—has this covered. How wonderful to know that He does. Yes, you might be scared. Yes, you might face the unknown with blinders on and have to wonder what's around the bend, but God will go with you, hand in hand.

Take heart! You are filled with energy for the tasks ahead! Change doesn't stop you in your tracks. You embrace it. You even look forward to it because you trust the One who has orchestrated it all.

YOU ARE ABLE TO SLOW THINGS DOWN

Do your best to present yourself to God as one approved,
a worker who does not need to be ashamed and
who correctly handles the word of truth.

2 TIMOTHY 2:15 NIV

Perhaps it's because we live in such an "instantaneous" world that we feel the need to get things done in a hurry. We certainly don't like anything to slow us down, especially lack of knowledge on our part. But moving at such a rapid pace 24-7 isn't good. . .for your body, your mind, or your spirit.

Maybe you can relate to Christie's story: She was the quintessential soccer mom, right down to the minivan. Her days were spent buzzing from her full-time job at a law firm to picking the kids up from school to the various practices. Just when she thought things couldn't get any busier, her daughter tried out for the school play. . .and got a lead role. The entire family ended up getting involved—making costumes, building set pieces, working backstage. Whew! Christie could hardly think straight because of the exhaustion. The week of the big show, everyone in the family cratered. They all ended up sick, and likely from exhaustion. Still, the show must go on. They forged ahead, but once the curtain was drawn on the final performance, Christie knew she could never allow a repeat of this fiasco. Something had to give. Next time they couldn't juggle sports and a show at the same time. No way!

Feel like you've walked a mile—or driven a mile—in Christie's shoes? Maybe you're reading this devotion on the go because you're overcommitted. Maybe you wish you had time to savor the time you spend in the Bible or in prayer, but you're so swamped it seems impossible.

What's it going to take to slow down, woman of purpose? What do you need to do—or give up—in order to make that happen? If you've been overcommitted with the kids, bouncing from soccer practice to ballet class, then perhaps it's time to have a heart-to-heart with your family about what's realistic. If you've been up to your eyeballs with volunteer work (at church or civic organizations), then perhaps a season of respite is called for. While it's great to serve, learning to say no can be very freeing.

Make up your mind to stop the madness. Stop the rush. There are only twenty-four hours in a day. That's true. But you won't enjoy any of them if you're buzzing through life at such a rapid pace. So put the brakes on! Then watch as God ministers to you as things s-l-o-w down. The Lord's voice is much easier to hear in the stillness than in the mad, rush-about seasons.

YOU ARE NOT CONFORMED TO THIS WORLD

Do not conform to the pattern of this world,
but be transformed by the renewing of your mind.
Then you will be able to test and approve what
God's will is—his good, pleasing and perfect will.

ROMANS 12:2 NIV

If you've ever worked a potter's wheel, you know what it's like to shape something into an image. You start with a lump of clay—no form, no shape. Then you work it into something that will hold water. Or food. Or into something beautiful to look at.

To "shape" something into an image is a good thing when you're talking about a potter's wheel, but it's not always a good thing when you're talking about shaping people into a certain image. Take Janet's story. As a teen, she desperately wanted to fit in. She tried with the kids at church, but they didn't seem to notice her. All of her would-be friends at school were from a rougher crowd, but she wanted their attention—good or bad. She started the "acceptance game" by joining them as they smoked cigarettes. From there, she moved to drinking, then drugs. Before long, she was hardly recognizable as the sweet kid she'd once been. Why? Because she'd allowed those around her to squeeze her into their mold, to force her into their image. Sadly, she not only allowed it, she wanted it. In the end, however, she didn't like the person she had become. Undoing years of "molding" took time and

effort, but she finally worked herself to a better place, free and clean. She would be the first to tell you that trying to fit in wasn't worth it. In fact, it almost destroyed her.

Why do we want to be like others? To look like them? To act like them? Why do we allow ourselves to morph and transform into something we're not even comfortable with? Because there's an innate desire within us to be loved. We even do this in churches, don't we? We put on our happy faces and pretend things are great, even when we're secretly hurting. And all so that we can look like happy-go-lucky Christian women who seem to have it all together.

There's only one image that we should allow ourselves to be shaped into, and that's Christ's. When we submit ourselves to looking, acting, conforming to His will, the end result is a lot prettier. And healthier. And happier. So don't allow yourself to be squeezed into a mold that isn't meant for you. The Lord has something far greater in mind for you. His "mold" is one of love, one that never makes you feel "squeezed" and always leaves you feeling better in the end.

YOU HAVE A PLACE IN THE BODY OF CHRIST

So it is with Christ's body. We are many parts of one body,
and we all belong to each other.

ROMANS 12:5 NLT

Some are hands. Some are feet. Some are lips. . .and so on. We've all got a place in the body of Christ, though not every woman feels that way.

Where do you fit in? Are you vivacious, ready, and willing to speak up? To direct the Christmas play? To teach a Bible study? To lead the women's ministry? Maybe you're a "mouth." Are you the sort of person who loves to care for those in need? Do you run to those who need help, providing meals or visiting people in the hospital? Maybe you're the "feet." Are you ready, willing, and able to roll up your sleeves and get your hands dirty? Ready to scrub toilets or help decorate the Sunday school rooms? Maybe you're the "hands."

The point is, there's a place for all of us! Sometimes it's just a matter of finding your perfect fit. And don't give up if you can't figure it out all at once. Learn from Tabitha, who tried it all! She started in the children's ministry, working with the little ones. After a few weeks, she was ready to admit defeat. After all, she already had three small children of her own. Working with kids on Sundays added to her frustration. So she switched gears and offered to cook meals for families in crisis. Only one problem with that—she wasn't a great cook. The stresses that came with having to prepare meals for her own family and other people besides almost

did her in. Tabitha switched gears again, this time offering to teach a Sunday school class for the teens. It didn't take long to figure out that teaching wasn't her thing. Putting together the lessons, standing up in front of the class. . .it exhausted her and left her feeling frazzled, not happy. More and more, Tabitha found herself in a place where others came to her for counsel. Ultimately, she joined the prayer team, realizing her real "gifting" was caring and praying for others.

Have you "played the circuit" at your church, like Tabitha? If so, you've likely figured out where you *don't* fit. Some things are pretty obvious. Figuring out where you *do* fit is something else altogether. Once you've found your sweet spot, you don't have to stress anymore. Finding your place in the body—whether you're an eye, an ear, a hand, a foot. . .or whatever—puts you in the perfect position to minister to others without bringing added stresses to yourself.

Aren't you glad you're part of something bigger than yourself? And aren't you glad you're needed? That's the thing about a "body." Every part is necessary to the whole! So find your perfect fit, and watch God work through you!

YOU'RE WINNING THE WAR AGAINST ANXIETY

Do not be anxious about anything, but in every
situation, by prayer and petition, with thanksgiving,
present your requests to God.

PHILIPPIANS 4:6 NIV

Oy! Anxiety! We wring our hands, anticipating the worst. We lay in bed at night, wondering how the bills will get paid. We pace the halls, our hearts racing, wondering if we will lose our job. We fret over everything from the kids' grades in school to our relationships with those we love. The inability to let go of our fears and worries can be crippling at times, but it's so hard to release them, especially if worrying has become a habit.

Maybe you're going through a life-altering situation right now. Perhaps you're struggling with a major health issue or the loss of a loved one. Perhaps you're going through a marital breakup or dealing with a prodigal child. No doubt you're struggling with inner turmoil. Maybe your nervous behaviors are ruling the day. Perhaps you're battling feelings of dread, even. You feel as if something is going to happen. . .possibly soon. You can't bear it, and you can't stop fretting.

Did you realize there's a huge difference between fear and anxiety? With fear, you're anticipating something that is likely to happen. Anxiety often builds up over "perceived" (not likely to happen) problems. Interesting, right?

So what's stressing you out today? Take a giant step back from this situation and ask yourself, "Is it *really likely* to happen, or is it more *unlikely* to happen?" Chances are, you're all worked up. . .for nothing. What has you wound up tighter than a knot probably isn't going to take place.

Take Brittany's story. After hearing that her best friend's husband lost his job, she grew anxious that her own husband might lose his as well. No, the two men didn't work for the same company. They weren't even in the same field. But this "perceived" threat of a job loss made her a nervous wreck. For days—weeks, even—she fretted over what the family would do if/when this happened. It never did. After several months went by, she relaxed and eventually forgot to worry anymore. After a while, she wondered why she'd ever fretted in the first place. In a sense, she'd taken on someone's struggle and made it her own.

Have you ever reacted like Brittany? Ever fretted over something that, in reality, probably wasn't going to happen? If so, then take another look at today's Bible verse: "Do not be anxious about anything." So, deep breath. Ask yourself, "Do I really have a reason to be wound up, or am I fretting over a perceived threat?" If it's a "likely to happen" situation, then the answer from God is still the same: "Don't worry!" And if it's a "not likely to happen" situation, you're wasting precious hours (and possibly your health) by fretting. So be free! Let it go and trust that God can give you a peace that passes understanding, no matter what you're facing.

YOU RISE TO THE OCCASION

I can do all things through Christ who strengthens me.
PHILIPPIANS 4:13 NKJV

Rising to the occasion. We're not always sure we can do it. Maybe you can relate. Perhaps you've been given an opportunity to speak before a large group and you're shaking in your boots. Maybe you find yourself in a one-on-one position where you feel a nudge to pray with a friend. . . but you're scared. How do you broach the subject? Will she let you?

Rising to the occasion isn't always easy, but it's always worth it in the end. Sure, it often requires courage, but remember where courage comes from. You don't have to summon it up. It's already inside of you, through the person of Jesus Christ.

It takes courage to confront your fears. It takes courage to face danger (or perceived danger), to look it in the eye. Even those "uncertain" times require a lot of courage because you don't know what's coming around the next bend, and that can be intimidating. (We women love to know what's coming, don't we?) Sometimes you have to summon up courage to do (or say) the right thing when others around you are cratering or bowing to pressure. No, it's not fun, but it's always right.

Consider Nadia's story: She started a business, and tax season rolled around. She knew that paying her taxes would be an issue, being self-employed, but didn't realize just how high the price tag would be until everything was documented. Ouch! Turned out she owed a lot

of money. A good friend suggested she tweak her tax return a bit to show more expenses. This same friend also shared that Nadia could withhold information about what she'd been paid in cash. This idea sounded very appealing, since doing so would bring her "taxes owed" amount down quite a bit. But in the end, she knew it wouldn't be right. So she squared her shoulders, faced her fear about the taxes, and did the right thing. She filed her taxes, set up a payment plan, and made sure she did a better job the following year. In other words, she rose to the occasion, even though it was tough. Facing her fears gave her the courage to grow, to become a better businesswoman, and the payoff was a moral/emotional one.

Surely you've faced seasons where you had a choice to either slink away or, like Nadia, square your shoulders and do the right thing. Slinking away is never a good option. You don't accomplish anything this way. You won't develop or grow if you hide from the problems, after all. So face them head on. Rise, rise, rise to the occasion. Stand tall and strong, even if the challenges are daunting.

Go ahead. Take a deep breath and dive in. You can do it, woman of purpose! You can stand when you need to stand, take a step when you need to take a step, and even do the very thing you think you cannot do. . .all with His strength.

YOUR WORDS MATTER

The words you say will either acquit you or condemn you.

MATTHEW 12:37 NLT

Words matter. In fact, they matter so much that the Lord tells us in His Word (the Bible) that the power of life and death is in the tongue. Ouch! With the same mouth we speak life (praises, joy, comfort) and death (insult, critique, anger). This should not be so. Still, we battle our words on a daily basis. The kids start fighting and we dive in, temper mounting. A coworker spouts off and we kick back, then regret it later. Oh, if only we could do a better job controlling our tongues!

Do you struggle with what comes out of your mouth? If so, then you'll appreciate Eliana's story. She fought a constant battle with critique. Raised in a home with parents who felt the need to nit-pick, she picked up the habit of offering advice. . .freely. Maybe a little too freely. When Eliana was with her friends, she would offer unsolicited advice, and not always in the most positive, upbeat fashion. She critiqued her children, her spouse, her coworkers, and sometimes in a public and humiliating way. Sometimes her words contained a "bite," and though she didn't mean to hurt others, she often did.

When Eliana entered into a relationship with the Lord, she came under conviction about her tongue. She decided to try an experiment—surrendering her words to the Lord for thirty days. No shouting. No critiques. No biting comments. It was hard—and sometimes she slipped

up—but after thirty days of living this way, people began to take notice. So did Eliana. She replaced her harsh words with carefully thought-out ones, and before long she realized that her change in attitude was affecting her own heart, even more than those around her.

What words do you need to stop using today? Do you tend to offer critique? Are your words laced with sarcasm? Do you raise your voice with your kids? These three things (critique, sarcasm, and temper) should be considered our mortal enemies. But how do you go about stopping? Put a plan in action. Write it down. Give yourself a timeframe: For thirty days I will not raise my voice with the kids. For two weeks I will not respond sarcastically to my coworkers. When you're on a timetable, you'll be more likely to stick with it. But don't do it because of the timetable. Do it because it's the right thing, because it makes God happy. Guarding your tongue will free you up to be a better witness to your coworkers, your children, and, yes, even your spouse.

The tongue can be your best friend when lovely words are allowed to roll off of it. So consider it—and those words—your best tool for reaching others with the love of Christ.

YOU FACE EACH MOUNTAIN WITH COURAGE

Truly I tell you, if anyone says to this mountain,
"Go, throw yourself into the sea," and does not
doubt in their heart but believes that what they
say will happen, it will be done for them.

MARK 11:23 NIV

Picture this. . .you're walking down the sidewalk, minding your own business, when suddenly—out of nowhere—a mountain appears in front of you. You stare at it, scratch your head, then try to figure out how to get to the other side. Maybe you could walk around it. Or maybe you could tunnel through it. Perhaps you could even climb it.

Then, just as you decide that none of those options sounds doable, you're reminded of something you read in the Bible. You can speak to the mountain. That's right. . .just tell it to be tossed into the sea!

Okay, maybe this analogy about a mountain has you shrugging. You haven't faced any literal ones lately. But maybe you've faced a few emotional ones. Perhaps you've stood at the bedside of a friend or loved one facing a cancer diagnosis. Maybe you've struggled through the breakup of a relationship. Perhaps you have experienced something traumatic—the loss of a home or the unexpected end of your business. These life obstacles are, in a sense, mountains that you've faced.

So, how does one handle a mountain. . .really? Sure, you could look at it and panic. Who would blame you? You could cry (which is completely

moment. As God spoke the waters into their very existence—as the waves rocked and reeled for the first time across the sand, the very Spirit of God moved, moved, moved. And as God set the sun up in the sky, as the shimmers of red, gold, and orange warmed the breeze on that first glorious morning, God's Spirit danced across it all, a lyrical ballet, majestic and triumphant.

Such an idea overwhelms us, fills us with wonder. We're awestruck by something so incredible, so breathtaking. The very word *creation* sets our hearts ablaze. Only God has the power to create! Only His Spirit can hover, dwell, and dance above it all.

Why is this so important to you, woman of purpose? Because the same Spirit lives in you! And you—God's finest creation—are more glorious than any sunset, than any rollicking ocean wave, than any brilliantly colored canyon. You are the best of the best, God's beloved. So, as you take in that next lovely scenic moment, remember that its beauty, no matter how breathtaking, doesn't hold a candle to you. Gorgeous in His sight, you are. More precious than the diamonds. More glorious than the setting sun. More magnificent than the tallest mountain. Go ahead. Relish in the beauty of nature. But while you're at it, don't forget to thank your Creator for creating the most wonderful thing of all—you, His child.

YOU ARE GIFTED

If you, then, though you are evil, know how to give good
gifts to your children, how much more will your Father
in heaven give good gifts to those who ask him!

MATTHEW 7:11 NIV

Remember what it was like on Christmas morning when you were a child?
Likely, you raced to the Christmas tree, eyes wide, as you took in all of
the beautifully wrapped gifts. You waited your turn, finally opening that
first present. Then the second. Then the third. All the while, your heart
raced. You could hardly believe your good fortune to get that new toy.
That new game. That new pair of pajamas. Those cool video games. It
seemed too good to be true.

Do you realize that God—the ultimate gift giver—has bestowed far
more on you than you could ever find under a Christmas tree? He's
given you gifts that can be used to reach others for the kingdom. Not
convinced? Look at Joyce's story. She grew up in a house with talented
people on every side. Her parents were both musicians. So were her
sisters. Even her younger brother excelled in music. The family traveled
from church to church, singing and playing their instruments. They
brought great joy to hundreds, if not thousands, of people over the
years. In the middle of it all, Joyce! From the time she was two, she
had a microphone in her hand, singing, singing, singing. She got over
her stage fright at an early age and took to the music scene with great

abandon. Her parents recognized a "gifting" in her and tapped into it, giving her plenty of opportunities.

What about you, woman of purpose? Where do your gifts lie? Don't say you don't have any. We all do! Maybe it's time to do a little inventory. Perhaps you're good at caring for the needy or offering love to someone who's hurting. Perhaps you have musical abilities or the desire to teach a class at your church. Maybe you're one of the few who can provide a meal for shut-ins or clothes for the local shelter. There are thousands of ways you can use your gifts to benefit others.

If you haven't used your gifts in a while, ask the Lord to give them a good stir. That's scriptural, you know. Picture God reaching down with a huge spoon—a ladle, even—and stirring, stirring, stirring your gifts, bringing them to the surface so that they are usable. He will do it if you ask, and then open yourself up to the possibilities. Just ask, then watch as He provides opportunity after opportunity to be used for the Kingdom.

Gifts. They're far more than what you find under the Christmas tree or on your birthday. They're sent down from on high to be given away again and again and again. What are you waiting for, woman of purpose? Unwrap those gifts!

YOU CAN RECOVER FROM LIFE'S TRAGEDIES

Dear brothers and sisters, when troubles of any kind come
your way, consider it an opportunity for great joy.

JAMES 1:2 NLT

Have you ever been through a tragedy so catastrophic that recovery felt impossible? Perhaps you struggled to pull yourself out of an emotional pit or situation. There's good news for you today: God can restore you to a place of normalcy and peace. You can—and will—recover from the rough season you've walked through. It's not up to you to make things better either. It's solely God's job to turn things around. Still, He wants your participation in the process, no doubt about it. If you're having a rough time, choose to praise Him anyway, even if it seems difficult.

Maybe you're like Katie. She found it difficult to praise God after walking through an earth-shaking event in her life. When Katie's best friend was diagnosed with pancreatic cancer, it felt like a bad dream. Katie held on tightly to the Lord's hand as her beloved friend bravely fought the good fight. Back and forth she went to the hospital, watching with horror as things progressed from bad to worse. She tried to keep a godly perspective, but with her friend in such agony, it felt impossible at times. When the moment to let go of her friend's hand came, Katie did her best to believe that God had a bigger plan. Several weeks after her best friend's death, however, Katie began to slip. Her faith waned. Her desire to praise, to celebrate life, to see the best in the situation just sort

of disappeared. In other words, she gave up. For the moment, anyway.

Eventually, the fog lifted. Katie was able to see a shift in her perspective. Life morphed to a new version of normalcy. She began to listen to worship music and found herself feeling more hopeful. No, her attitude didn't change overnight. She was still confused. Still bothered by the fact that God—who could have healed her friend—had chosen not to, at least in the way Katie had hoped.

Tragedies mark us. They leave an imprint. But they don't have to ground us. Life really does go on, even after the most horrific events. And while it might not seem right that the sun goes on shining, it does. That sun is a symbol that we too can see brighter days ahead. It will take time, of course, but things will get better. The Lord will walk with you every step of the way, His hand gently leading you past the fog toward a more hopeful season.

YOU ARE AN ENCOURAGEMENT TO OTHERS

Therefore encourage one another and build
each other up, just as in fact you are doing.

1 Thessalonians 5:11 niv

Encouraging people are such a blast to be around. They give you hope when you're feeling blue, they offer a pat on the back when you need encouragement, and they show up at just the right time when you need a shoulder to cry on.

Callie, a young wife and mother, was a terrific encourager to her friends. Everyone knew just who to call when they needed a kind word or compassionate hug. She was happy to oblige. She garnered the nickname "Cheerful Callie" because of her positive spin on life and the never-ending smile on her face. Then, things began to fall apart for Callie. Her husband lost his job. Her children began to struggle in school. She tried to remain encouraging to others but found it difficult. And who could she turn to? Everyone came to her, not the other way around. She had to be strong. . .for them.

So, Callie tried to pretend everything was fine. She put on a happy (albeit forced) smile, stiffened her backbone, and kept focused on others, never confessing her need to her friends and family members. For a while, things went okay. She said the usual encouraging things to others but secretly wished someone would give her a pat on the back. She quoted scripture to friends but wondered if those same words

would ever penetrate her heart again. Eventually a good friend picked up on the "real" Callie, the one she wasn't showing to others. With that friend's help, Callie found comfort and healing, though it took her a while to open up and truly share her heart. After all, sharing the icky stuff (to her way of thinking) might ruin her "too good to be true" testimony.

Oh sweet woman of purpose. . .don't you see? Encouragement works both ways! We are called to be an encouragement, yes, but we're all called to receive encouragement when the situation calls for it. So, sure, be a "Cheerful Callie." But when things around you are crumbling, don't put on your game face. Don't pretend that everything is perfect when it's not. People want to see the real you so that they can give you the encouragement you need when you need it. And let's face it, our testimony isn't ruined when we get gut-honest about things. In fact, it's strengthened because people see us as a real person who has struggles. A person who overcomes, with the Lord's help.

Get real. Those two words are more than just a passing phrase. Get real, woman of purpose. In doing so, you will become the greatest encouragement of all.

YOU PRESS ON

Not that I have already obtained all this,
or have already arrived at my goal, but I press on to
take hold of that for which Christ Jesus took hold of me.

PHILIPPIANS 3:12 NIV

Picture this: You're having new floors put in, so you move the furniture out to the garage until the process is over. It's been quite an exhausting process already, but there's still work to be done. When you're ready to bring the sofa back inside, it gets lodged in the door—half in and half out. Now what? You're stuck. So you push. And push, and push some more. Finally! That last nudge does the trick. You break past the hurdle and the sofa slides on through.

That might sound like a funny example, but sometimes life presents "stuck" moments like that. We're half in, half out, and not sure which way to go. . .forward or backward. When you're a woman of purpose—when you feel the drive and zeal of the Lord—you don't give up, even when you've pushed for hours! (Perhaps this devotion is conjuring up images of being in labor! Surely many of you can relate.) The point is, some things are worth pushing for. And once you get past the hurdle, the rest, as they say, is downhill. And going backward? It's never a good idea. Pressing forward is just that—pressing forward, toward something new. Unknown. Exciting.

So, what are you "pressing/pushing" toward today? What are you

hoping to accomplish? Have you set dieting goals? Are you working your way up the corporate ladder? Trying to get your house organized? Maybe you can't see around the next bend. And sure, you might feel frozen in place at times, but don't give up. Whatever you're facing, do it with gusto. When you get stuck—and you surely will—give a strong push. If you don't break free all at once, don't give up! Keep pressing! Keep pushing! In short order you will get beyond the hurdle and your pace will pick up.

Remember, <u>half of the journey is in the mind.</u> You've got to have a "never give up" attitude. Stick with it. And remember today's scripture: whatever you're pushing toward, Christ has already taken hold of you. Whew! That makes the journey easier, doesn't it!

YOU ARE BLESSED TO BE YOU

For you created my inmost being;
you knit me together in my mother's womb.

PSALM 139:13 NIV

Have you ever spent a full day praising God for making you. . .you? As women, we often look at others and long to be like them. We say things like, "If only I had her body!" or, "Wow, I would love to have a marriage like hers." Comments like, "Wow, her hair is so much nicer than mine. I'd love to have curls" tumble from our lips, unrehearsed. Instead of focusing on our unique design or our individual blessings, we long to be like others.

Take Lisa's story, for instance. She always felt cheated. All of the other girls were pretty. She felt like a Plain Jane in comparison. The other girls had talents. She felt like a hopeless nobody. While others were courageous and filled with energy, she just wanted to hide away from the crowd and read a book. Or two. Or twelve. Even in the stories, she felt defeated. The characters in the novels appeared to be perfect— swashbuckling heroes, blissful damsels, and plenty of romance for all.

When Lisa finally realized that God had created her in His image, she stopped comparing herself to others and asked Him to spotlight areas of her life where she could grow and develop. He did! Before long, she felt more content with her appearance, more grateful for her quirks (even the flaws) and more at peace with who—and how—she had

been crafted by the Lord.

Can you relate to Lisa's issues? Maybe you don't feel particularly lovely, inside or out. It's time to "get rid of your stinkin' thinkin' " (as your mama would say) and change your attitude. How do you go about that? Here are a few ideas:

Take a day to write down the reasons you feel blessed to be you. Maybe your list would look something like this: "I'm blessed to be healthy. Thank You, God, for my family. I'm grateful for my children. Father, bless You for giving me a place to live. I'm so thrilled to have a home/apartment. I'm blessed with good food to eat. I'm grateful for my job. I'm thankful that You show up in the middle of my distresses, Lord. Thank You for helping me overcome life's temptations. What a blessing, to have the Lord on my side when I'm going through trials." Writing things down helps so much because it forces us to see the good, and there's a lot of good to be seen!

No one has a perfect life. Or a perfect body. No one is perfectly gifted or overly talented. Most of us are insecure, at best. But when we take the time to express gratitude for our uniqueness, everything comes into perspective.

YOU CAN GIVE SOFT ANSWERS

A soft answer turns away wrath,
but a harsh word stirs up anger.

PROVERBS 15:1 ESV

"Temper, temper!" Maybe you grew up hearing those words. The tendency to flare up can start in early childhood and carry on into our adult lives if we don't "temper" ourselves. And those flare-ups can hurt a lot of people, including those you love. We don't set out to hurt them, of course, but it happens, just the same. The desire to live calm, steady lives is there, but we don't know how to take the first step. We seem to pop our cork instead.

Lorie knew what it was like to battle her temper. She always seemed to blow her top when things went wrong. She spewed on her husband, her kids, the ladies in her Bible study—pretty much everyone she came in contact with. It wasn't until Lorie got into private counseling sessions that she realized the truth: Her temper was rooted in a deep-seated, yet-unspoken anger at a teacher who had ridiculed her in front of the class. The situation still hurt whenever she thought about it, though she never shared the story publicly. Instead of lashing out at the person who had hurt her (and let's face it, victims almost never do because they're so afraid), she let the emotions build up. Unspoken pain winds itself around the heart and binds us up, but there's usually an explosion in the end!

In some ways, Lorie's temper issues could be traced back to another

person, a specific incident. But here's the joy in letting go of pain, in offering forgiveness: When you let it go, the person you end up helping is yourself. Holding onto pain, refusing to offer forgiveness, only serves to get you wound up on the inside. And it's only a matter of time before you blow.

Think of anger like a can of biscuits. It doesn't take much for the can to "pop" open and for biscuits to go flying all over the room. Just one little sliver of air and the whole can explodes. That's what happens when pressure builds up on the inside of you. So, if you're battling temper issues, ask the Lord to show you what it is you're really struggling with. Once He's revealed it, pray about that situation, that person, that obstacle. . .and then let it go. If you do, the can of biscuits sits safely on the counter, not hurting a soul. If you don't. . .watch out! The explosion could get messy! You'll end up with biscuits on the wall, the ceiling, the floor, and a thousand other places besides.

YOU TAKE PLEASURE IN LIFE

How we thank God for you! Because of you
we have great joy as we enter God's presence.
1 THESSALONIANS 3:9 NLT

Life is hard! Just one more reason why you need to enjoy the little things, to relish in the beauty of nature, to dance a little jig when things are going well. God longs for us to enjoy His creation, to take pleasure in life. The problem is, we're often so caught up in the day-to-day drama of "existing" that we forget to really, truly live. To let our hair down. To dance in rain puddles and skip through fields of clover.

Here are some fun ways you can break outside your shell and start to enjoy life more: Take pictures. Photography offers a fantastic way to intricately examine nature from an up close and personal point of view. Through the lens of your camera you will see details as you've never seen them before—the butterfly's wings, the flower's nectar, the dew on the morning grass. Observing nature from this vantage point will draw you closer to the Lord and set your heart ablaze with praise for His creation.

Here are a couple of other suggestions: Be in the moment. When you're with friends or loved ones, really be with them. Put your cell phone away. Don't respond to texts or calls unless they're critical. Listen closely to those you're with. Invest your time. You will find that you're not thinking ahead to the next event on your calendar if you're truly

invested in the person you're with. And you will find pleasure in little things, like quiet conversation, a cup of hot tea, or a yummy cookie shared with a loved one.

Why do we often miss the little things? Why does life not seem as pleasurable as it should? Because we're rushing, rushing, rushing to the next event, the next obligation, the next person. Only when we pause to enjoy the moments do we experience pleasure. So, the next time you take a bite of a gooey chocolate chip cookie, slow down and enjoy it. Don't shovel it down. That next morning walk through your neighborhood? Don't spend it thinking about all of the day's obligations. Look at what's in front of you—the fluffy clouds in the pristine sky, the pink flowers blooming in your neighbor's garden, the darling puppy staring at you out of your neighbor's window.

When you pause to drink in these little things, pleasure always follows. And don't you imagine that's how it is with the Lord too? Can't you picture Him looking down from heaven at you, His heart filled with pleasure as He takes in the little details—your messy hair, the mismatched socks, the smile on your face? If God takes pleasure in us, we can surely pause long enough to take pleasure in His creation. He made it all for you, you know!

Who, then, is this person that fears the LORD? He is the
one whom the LORD will teach which path to choose.

PSALM 25:12 GW

Choices. Most women have a love/hate relationship with them. Before it's time to make one, you strategize. You make up your mind. Then, in the moment, you crater. Oy! What a dilemma.

Take Eliza's story, for instance. She worked so hard to take off thirty pounds. She worked out, trimmed back on calories, drank gallons of water, and preached her healthy eating lifestyle on social media. Anyone who was anyone knew better than to tempt Eliza with sugary sweets. Not that she would have eaten them anyway. No, with her resolve firmly in place, she would go on making wise, healthy choices. . .for the rest of her life.

And then Thanksgiving came around. She took a few nibbles of some not-so-great-for-her foods. No big deal, right? Well, no big deal until Christmas unveiled like a sugary gift in front of her, loaded with cookies, cakes, and every good thing. It started so innocently. Just a couple of cookies here. A piece of pie there. A sampling of that yummy French toast casserole at a Christmas brunch. And then there were the church Christmas parties. Everyone expected her to bake her yummy cake pops, so she did. Of course, she had to sample them while baking to make sure they were good.

Before long, Eliza's choices were shifting, along with her resolve. After Christmas she faced the bathroom scale, horrified to see that she'd gained ten pounds. Ouch! She had no one to blame but herself, and blame she did. She carried a shroud of guilt that weighted her down even more. Instead of propelling her to do the right thing, that guilt caused her to give up altogether. She saw herself as a dieting failure.

Can you relate to Eliza's woeful tale? Most of us plan to do the right thing. Our intentions are good. Then, in the moment, we make a not-so-great choice. Instead of brushing ourselves off, we get into an "Oh, well. I've already blown it" mentality. . .and continue to slip. And slip. And slip some more. Doesn't matter what area of life we're talking about here, we can brush ourselves off and begin again. Yesterday's failures don't matter. . .at all.

Today is a fresh day! Purpose in your heart to make wise, healthy, good choices, not just with your eating, but in every area of your life. All that really matters is what's in front of you at this very moment. So tread carefully! Choose wisely. You can do this, woman of purpose! You are not a failure. You have blissful days ahead, thanks to wise choices today.

YOU ARE WORTHY OF LOVE

And so we know and rely on the love God has for us. God is love. Whoever lives in love lives in God, and God in them.

1 JOHN 4:16 NIV

Have you ever felt like you weren't lovable? Maybe you're not the cuddle-up-and-give-me-a-kiss sort. Or maybe you are, but there's no one around to offer that sort of affection. Perhaps you've walked a rough road and your past—the sins you committed ages ago—is haunting you. Because of those sins, you don't feel worthy of love, so you push others (and possibly God) aside, rejecting them before they can (supposedly) reject you. How sad to live a life without the love of others to comfort you!

Here's good news, woman of purpose! God adores you, and He doesn't question your worth. Not only are you worthy of His love, that unconditional "I love You!" extended all the way to the cross, where His Son gave up His life for you. Wow! Even in your unworthiness, Jesus was willing to carry your sin, your shame, to Calvary.

Paula carried a lot of hidden shame. In her former life she'd been really promiscuous. In fact, her promiscuity had led to not one pregnancy, but two. Her children had never known their respective fathers, and she didn't talk much about it, even when she gave her heart to the Lord and eventually married a wonderful, godly man. Still, her past haunted her. She didn't feel like the other ladies in the group at church. So she kept her mouth shut and put on a sweet smile, hiding her past. Whenever

she came across verses about worthiness, she cringed. She didn't feel worthy of God's love, not even on the best of days. It took a breakthrough (which happened during a women's retreat) to come to grips with her past and to see that God still loved her, no matter what she'd done. When she finally let go of the shame, Paula began to see herself as worthy of God's love. . .for the first time. How freeing! How blissful!

Have you walked a mile in Paula's shoes? Sure, there will still be days when you don't feel worthy. Welcome to the club. And there will be days when you don't feel like loving others. When those days come, ask God to give you His heart. He doesn't base love on feelings, and neither should you. Push those feelings aside and settle into his never-ending, doesn't-matter-how-life-is-treating-you, doesn't-matter-what-mistakes-you've-made-today brand of love.

YOU ARE ONE STEP CLOSER TODAY

God again set a certain day, calling it "Today." This he
did when a long time later he spoke through David,
as in the passage already quoted: "Today, if you
hear his voice, do not harden your hearts."

HEBREWS 4:7 NIV

If you've ever run a marathon, you know the value of pacing yourself. If you set your sites on accomplishing the whole thing, you'll surely fail. If you take it in bite-sized chunks, you're more likely to make it to the finish line.

The same principle is true with many things in life—dieting, for instance. Let's say you want to lose forty pounds. If you set your sites on the forty pounds, you'll get discouraged. Every one- or two-pound loss will seem minimal in comparison. So you have to set tiny goals, five or ten pounds at a time.

No one understood this better than Renata. She wanted to run in a local marathon to raise money for breast cancer awareness, something her mother had suffered through. Not really much of a runner, Renata started small. She didn't push off her first run till "tomorrow." She started "today." She didn't feel like it but decided feelings had nothing to do with it.

First, she focused on making it around the block. Then, she slowly "grew" her distance until she could run a 5k. By the time the race day

came, she knew she could make it to the finish line because she'd worked herself up to it. No, it wouldn't be easy. Yes, it would be doable. What made it possible? She'd paced herself. She hadn't tried to bite off huge chunks. Instead, she'd worked in increments. Piecing those increments together, she'd developed herself as a runner and had increased her stamina.

Maybe you want to run a marathon. Or bike ten miles. Or try out for the church's Christmas play. Or sing in the choir. Maybe you're not quite there yet and need to make progress. Learn from Renata. Take baby steps, a few at a time. Gradually work yourself up to where you need to be.

No matter where you are in your journey—spiritual, physical, or otherwise—you are definitely one step closer to your goal than you were yesterday. Even if you slipped and fell, you're one day closer. Even if you made mistakes yesterday, you're in a position today to move forward. Don't look back. Keep your eye on the prize. You can do this, woman of purpose. One foot in front of the other. Keep moving. Start today, so that you have no regrets tomorrow. Progress begins right now. Before long, you'll be running with ease and wondering why you ever doubted yourself!

YOUR MIND-SET CAN CHANGE

Let this mind be in you,
which was also in Christ Jesus.
PHILIPPIANS 2:5 KJV

Lindy grew up in a home where people talked about politics. . .a lot. She was taught to think a certain way about people, based on their political views. Sometimes the conversations got heated. Passionate. Lindy jumped onboard, loving the sense of unity she felt when others agreed with her. She felt strong. Fortified.

But, as the years ticked by, not everyone agreed with her. As she grew, Lindy ostracized friends and coworkers because of her strong stance. At first she didn't realize that people were avoiding her, but after a while she could deny it no longer. Lindy took a step back and prayed about her situation. She began to analyze her former mind-set, finally coming to grips with the idea that, perhaps, she didn't even really agree with her parents and their views. After much prayer and careful analysis, Lindy did the unthinkable—she changed her mind. She still had passionate beliefs, but this time they were rooted in her faith, in her own personal journey. They made sense to her.

Maybe you've walked a mile in Lindy's shoes. Perhaps you were raised in a particular denomination and took a strong stance, only to shift gears as an adult. You viewed life through a particular filter, only to watch that filter change with age. This is not to say that all denominations

(or political parties) are wrong. . .or bad. But our groups/beliefs have to line up with the Word of God and with what makes sense to us as individuals.

Here's the point: your mind-set can change. You don't have to remain hard-core in your stance, simply because that's what you've been raised to do. Ask God to show you His perspective, then be prepared for a bit of shifting! Your mind can change about a great many things. For instance, maybe you grew up with certain views about people of other races. God can—and likely will—change your mind about all of that. Maybe you grew up thinking that certain foods were icky. Then, as you aged, you fell in love with those foods. Perhaps you grew up despising exercise, only to discover a love of jogging as an adult.

There's one change that's bigger than all others combined. When you change your "I can handle life on my own" mind-set, God sweeps in and takes the reins. And when God's fully in control. . .watch out! A great many changes lie ahead. But don't fret. Change is a good thing, when the Lord is in it!

YOU CAN FIND THE GOOD

Search for good instead of evil so that you may live. Then the
LORD God of Armies will be with you, as you have said.

AMOS 5:14 GW

Finding the good. Sometimes it's tough! Picture this: you're walking
through a rough season. Perhaps you're going through a divorce or
breakup in a relationship. Your heart is broken. You wonder if you will
ever feel normal—or loved—again.

Sadie went through a rough patch. She was engaged to a great guy,
Ethan, straight out of Bible college. They had great plans for the future.
She could picture it all now. . .they would work together in ministry,
possibly even going on the mission field. They would have two or three
children and impact the world for the sake of the Gospel. Then, just five
weeks before the big day, her fiancé changed his mind. He didn't want
to get married anymore. He wasn't involved with anyone else; he just
felt the relationship/marriage wasn't God's will for his life. Sadie was, as
you might imagine, devastated. Her heart was broken. She questioned
everything, including her faith in God. Hadn't He orchestrated their
engagement in the first place?

Three painful years went by before Sadie met the man who would,
indeed, become her husband. No, he wasn't setting out for the mission
field. He worked as an engineer at an oil and gas company. But he was
God's perfect match for her. They married and had three beautiful

children, and she lived the life that the Lord had planned for her all along. Many times she whispered the "Thank You, God, that I did not marry Ethan!" prayer. And she meant it.

In the midst of such trauma it's hard to find the good, but God wants to restore your hope. Instead of dwelling on what was, or what might have been, why not focus on God's grace to get you through today? His plans for you are huge—far bigger than you could dream. He's got better things ahead. So, when things go wrong (and they will) just say to yourself, "God must have something greater in mind." He does, you know.

There's really only one way to find the good; you have to stop dwelling on the bad. Don't play the scenes over like a movie in your head. Don't keep rewinding and wishing, hoping, dreaming that you could change the past. It's over. Clip the film and start fresh. The photos, the images you need to focus on are the ones found in the Word of God. The Bible is filled with promises about hope. Joy. Peace. Restoration.

There is good in every situation. When you're heartbroken, you have a God who cares. When you're facing loss, God will fill you with His peace. When you're up against a financial struggle, you have a God who supplies all your needs. Think of yourself as an archaeologist. Keep searching, digging, scraping, hunting for the good. You will surely find it.

YOU CAN GET BEYOND THE SADNESS

Be merciful to me, LORD, for I am in distress; my eyes
grow weak with sorrow, my soul and body with grief.

PSALM 31:9 NIV

Navigating your way through a season of grief can be dreadful on many levels. In many ways it's like trying to make your way from one place to another in the dark of night, when you're not sure where you're going or what might be in your way. To get to the other side of such a difficult season, you have to do two things: 1) Trust that there is life beyond what you're walking through right now, and 2) Don't question God's goodness.

That second one is tough, especially if you feel the person you're mourning left this life before his time. Cynthia, a young mother, is a prime example. She lost her oldest child (who was only four) from a tragic illness. He died quickly, unexpectedly, after only being ill for a few days. This catastrophic loss rocked Cynthia's world, as you might imagine. She simply couldn't take it in. Afterward, she walked around in a fog. Her other children needed her, but she didn't have the wherewithal to care for them. Her husband stepped up to the plate and did the lion's share of the work, but he secretly wondered if he had lost his wife, as well as his child.

It took a long time to get to the point where she could function, even seminormally. To get back to a regular life felt like a betrayal to her firstborn. How could the sun go on shining without him? How could

she give her love to the others? It hardly seemed fair.

And yet, she did. And through loving the others, she finally grieved her way to a better place. Instead of arguing with God, she eventually learned to trust Him again. No, she didn't have all the answers, but she stopped asking the "Why?" question.

If you've grieved the loss of a loved one (or a relationship or a job), there is hope. You will get to a better place. The weeping won't go on forever. And though it may seem impossible, your heart will eventually beat evenly again. . .with God's help. No, things won't look the same. You will still battle emotions and feelings, which are God given. But you can trust the Lord in the very middle of your pain. He adores you and wants to see you comforted.

There is life beyond what you're walking through. There is. And, whether it feels like it or not, God is good. His love for you endures beyond all pain and sadness.

YOUR PERSPECTIVE MATTERS

May the God who gives endurance and encouragement
give you the same attitude of mind toward
each other that Christ Jesus had.

ROMANS 15:5 NIV

Endurance. We get tired just speaking the word! Abby came to understand that word all too well when she became a caregiver for her father. As her father's health declined, she made up her mind to keep a good attitude and to stick with it, no matter how tough the journey got. Knowing that her father was probably in his last few months of life, she wanted to make his days precious. Sure, there were days when she cried herself to sleep at night, but Abby didn't give up. She endured, even when things were really, really tough.

After three months of battling, her father passed away. Many people gathered around Abby and offered love and support. Others—his friends and extended family—offered multiple thanks to her for caring for her father in such a selfless way. A few acknowledged that they had watched her with great admiration. Several wise friends suggested she take some time for herself to recover physically and emotionally. Why was this so important? Because endurance is exhausting!

Maybe you're going through a season where you're being asked to endure. Maybe the journey seems too long. Too hard. Maybe the road seems hard to navigate. Don't give up. Put one foot in front of

the other and keep going. Your strength doesn't come from within, no matter what the "self-focused" crowd tells you. Your strength comes from on high, from the Lord Himself. He's right there with you, holding your hand and even carrying you during the hardest of times.

The runner who endures will approach the finish line and hear the words: "Well done, good and faithful servant." You can do this, woman of purpose. . .no matter how hard. With His help, you will make it. And the driving force? Your perspective. You can either have a "This is a dreadful season. Why do I have to go through this?" attitude, or you can have a "Thank You, God, for giving me the opportunity to draw closer to You and closer to those I love." The choice, though difficult at times, can make all the difference.

How do you define perspective? It's all about attitude, sister! It's your way of looking at the situation, your particular point of view. You can choose to be a woman of right perspective. Instead of feeling like giving up, you will be motivated, because you see things through a godly lens. So put on those spiritual glasses. Ask for God's point of view. Then endure the race with His vision.

YOU ARE NO LONGER IN BONDAGE

The Spirit you received does not make you slaves,
so that you live in fear again; rather, the Spirit you
received brought about your adoption to sonship.
And by him we cry, "Abba, Father."

ROMANS 8:15 NIV

Felicity didn't mean to struggle with an addiction to alcohol. In fact, she would have considered herself the least likely person to do so. After all, she'd grown up with an alcoholic father who couldn't pay the bills because of his addiction, who didn't know how to show love because of his volatile emotional state, and who ended up in the hospital time and time again with alcohol poisoning, liver damage, and a host of other self-induced ailments.

No, she didn't mean to get addicted to alcohol, but that's exactly what happened. As a youngster she vowed she'd never touch the stuff. It had ruined her father's life, after all. But as a young adult, she found herself tempted. After a few "innocent" drinks, she was hooked. Before long, she was completely in bondage to the stuff. Oh, she hid it well enough from others, but Felicity knew the truth. She couldn't make it from one day to the next without a drink. Or two. Or five. Before long, she didn't even care if her family and friends knew. What did it matter, anyway? She had her alcohol to keep her company and to bring comfort. Of course, it was a bittersweet friend, one that left her feeling empty and ill.

Maybe you can relate to Felicity's story. Perhaps you're in bondage to something too—alcohol; sugar; fried foods; gratuitous, extramarital sex. When you're in bondage, it's the equivalent of being seated in a chair with ropes tied around you. It seems as if there's no way out.

Oh, but there is a way out, woman of purpose! You can break free with God's help. No, you don't have the strength to do it yourself, but He's powerful enough to do the work. You just have to surrender to Him. When you do, He can—in one fell swoop—take those ropes and snap them. The bondage can come to its rightful end, replaced with a freedom you've never known.

Half the battle lies in the choosing. You must choose to be set free, and you have to mean it. You can't end an addition with a half-hearted, "wish I could change" attitude. You have to be all in. You must let one little six-letter word rule the day: D-E-C-I-D-E. Once the decision is truly made, the Spirit of God has the freedom to take the reins and do the necessary work. Submit to His plan, His will (no matter how hard), and watch as those ropes snap in two. Bondage can truly be a thing of the past. God calls you to live in complete and total freedom in Him.

YOUR HOPE IS IN THE LORD

We remember before our God and Father your work
produced by faith, your labor prompted by love, and your
endurance inspired by hope in our Lord Jesus Christ.

1 THESSALONIANS 1:3 NIV

Darla, a single woman in her thirties, prayed for years that she would someday own her own home. She hoped (in spite of obstacles) that she would one day settle into a place that was hers, one where she could choose to paint the walls whatever color she wanted. She hoped to find a place near her job. She hoped to invite friends from church over to her spacious kitchen, where they would share meals together. And so, she set out to make it happen, working extra hours to save money, then looking at house after house, ready to find the perfect one.

After settling on the ideal place, Darla made a solid offer. She knew beyond a shadow of a doubt that she would get the home of her dreams. Instead, she was devastated to receive news that her offer on the house was not accepted. Someone else placed a higher bid and had a more substantial income. She lost *her* house. The one she'd already begun to decorate in her imagination. The one she planned to live in for the rest of her life. Darla couldn't believe it. Her hopefulness ended in disappointment. She tucked away the desire to purchase and signed another lease agreement on her apartment.

Have you ever hoped for something, wished it would happen, only

to lose out? If so, then you surely understand Darla's heartbreak. Here's good news, in spite of any walls you've faced, in spite of any slammed doors, you can still put your hope and trust in God. You've heard the old adage: "If God closes a door, somewhere He opens a window." It's true! When doors close, (though it rarely feels like it in the moment), He always has a better plan.

Don't believe it? One year after Darla lost the home of her dreams, she met the man of her dreams. Robert owned his own home, one far greater than the house Darla was looking at. She married him, moved into the home, and they raised a family together. Along the way she learned to put her hope—not in a house—but in the Lord. God's plan for her was so much bigger than she could have dreamed.

Sure, things don't always work out like we want. And true, life can take its toll! We get disillusioned. Feel hopeless. But oh, sweet woman of purpose. . .if only we could see the bigger picture. If only we knew the blessings around the bend. Then none of the disappointments would matter one whit.

Trust Him. Put your hope in Him. You won't be disappointed.

YOUR JOY IS CONTAGIOUS

We are writing these things so
that you may fully share our joy.
1 JOHN 1:4 NLT

Poor Lisa! She lived in a house with three small children who always seemed to be sick. When one kiddo would catch a cold, she would pass it to the others. On and on it went. The word "contagious" became a steady part of Lisa's vocabulary. She found herself going back and forth to the pediatrician's office on multiple occasions, and always because the kids "shared" their illnesses. She turned to social media as an outlet of whining about how pitiful her life was. Nearly every post was a "woe is me" cry for attention. Sure, she wanted the prayers and support of others, but after a while, people turned a deaf ear, particularly when she began to criticize her husband's unwillingness to share the load. Sad, because she really needed the love and support of her friends and family. Instead of spreading a positive, hopeful message, she chose to wallow in the negative.

Think about that word *contagious* for a moment. It's an interesting word, isn't it? When you're contagious, you're pretty sure that others will "catch" what you have. This isn't good when you're ill, but it's wonderful when you're filled with joy. A joyous woman bubbles over and spreads her joy (good-for-you germs) with others! She giggles her way into the hearts of those around her and causes people to "catch" what she's got.

Before long, others are bubbling with joy too.

Where does this joy come from? It bubbles up inside of us when we realize our purpose. When we appreciate our design, our unique calling from the Lord. It dances in our hearts when we overcome obstacles and speak to mountains. It rushes over us like a mighty river when we witness miracles. It even settles deep into our hearts when we find healing after brokenness. In short, joy is a gift, one we couldn't conjure up, but one that becomes a part of our daily walk. No, we don't always walk through positive, upbeat times, but that doesn't mean our perspective has to sour. We don't have to sour others with our negativity. There's a choice to be made!

Are you a joyous person? If not, perhaps you need to spend more time with positive, upbeat people to "catch" the bug. Once you've caught it, there's no cure! Your job—should you choose to accept it—is to spread the bug to everyone you come in contact with. It's all about perspective, of course. You can choose to be joyous, even in the midst of the battle. When you do, watch out! Joy strengthens you! It gives you the wherewithal to power through, even when the struggle seems huge.

What are you waiting for? Catch the bug, woman of purpose. Then do your best to pass it on to everyone you come in contact with.

YOU ARE SURROUNDED BY BEAUTIFUL PEOPLE

Now you are the body of Christ,
and each one of you is a part of it.

1 CORINTHIANS 12:27 NIV

The world is filled with wacky, wonderful, unique people. They're tall, short, chubby, thin. . .and everything in-between. Each one is magnificently loved by his/her Creator. Doesn't matter where they live, what color their skin happens to be, or what language they speak. The love of God knows no social barriers. It sees past any physical flaws, any human barriers, any class systems.

When was the last time you paused to truly focus on the inward and outward beauty of the people around you? That elderly neighbor with her soft, wrinkled skin and ever-present smile. That mail carrier with the armload of envelopes. That passel of kiddos getting off the bus, their laughter ringing out across the street. The clerk at the grocery store, so preoccupied with her work that she barely glances your way as she rings up your order. That teenager in the parking lot, gabbing with her friends. That twenty-something guy with all the tattoos. Each one is beautiful in the eyes of his/her Creator.

To view others as beautiful requires God-sight. We need His vision. When He looks at flawed humankind, He sees each one through eyes of love. And not just any kind of love. His is the happily-ever-after, see-you-in-heaven-where-we'll-spend-eternity-together kind.

If anyone understood this, Mother Teresa did. She worked in the slums of Calcutta, tending to the needs of the orphaned children. Her love and passion for the downtrodden was relentless. She tended to those who were starving, the "poorest of the poor." Things weren't easy for her, as you might imagine, but she didn't give up. Sometimes she found herself begging for food and supplies, but she would not relent. From her passion came an organization—a small order of nuns—that grew to over four thousand. The word blossomed, eventually providing centers across the globe with hundreds of thousands cared for. All of this from one woman's quiet passion to help the poor.

Many would look at a photograph of Mother Teresa and think, *She wasn't very beautiful.* In fact, she wasn't, not by the world's standards. She dressed like the poor, didn't wear her hair in the latest fashion, and probably didn't own a pair of heels. Oh, but if the critics could only see the love in her heart, if they could catch a glimpse of the passion in her eyes, they might think again. Sometimes the "plainest" of people are the most gorgeous on the inside. Their beauty lies in the God-given desires and passions to spread love wherever they go.

Just something to ponder as you look into the eyes of those you come in contact with every day. You are, indeed, surrounded by beauty, woman of purpose.

YOU ARE SAFE IN HIS ARMS

The name of the LORD is a fortified tower;
the righteous run to it and are safe.

PROVERBS 18:10 NIV

Have you ever pondered the word *safe*? In baseball, a player is safe if he reaches a base before he's put out. In other words, he reaches his goal before the opponent forces him to quit. Think about that for a moment. We often face challenges. When we feel frightened, we often feel like quitting. When we "drop out" (emotionally, psychologically, spiritually) we feel like the game is over. There's no safety net.

Gillian knew what it meant to drop out. After facing an unexpected robbery at her workplace (a busy downtown bank), she froze in her tracks, grounded by fear. She quit her job and decided to work from home. Her doors stayed locked. She rarely went out with friends. She simply didn't feel safe anymore. It took some time before she braved being in public again, and even then she moved with great caution. Eventually she conquered her fear and got back to the business of living, but it took a long time.

Life offers plenty of opportunities to feel scared. And we're wise to move with caution, especially if we've been injured in the past. But fear is a funny thing. It's like a prison, complete with bars and locked door. Once inside, it's harder than ever to break free. And so we sit, completely frozen in place, wondering what it would be like to have a

real life, free from fear.

How do you get out of this prison cell? It takes courage. It takes trust, not in yourself, but in God's protection over your life. You have to examine that word *safe* in context with God's Word. You are safe under His umbrella. You are safe in His arms. You are safe to share your hurts, your pains, your fears.

Don't believe it? Think about your relationship with your children (or any youngsters in your life). Wouldn't you lay down your life to protect them? If they ran into a busy street, wouldn't you do everything in your power to save them? Imagine how much more your heavenly Father must want to protect you, to keep you safe. He adores you and has your best interest at heart. You mean the world to Him. And you can trust Him, just as the young child can trust his mother or father to race to his side in time of crisis.

Safe. Protected. It's the best way to live. So draw near to the One who longs to keep you that way, then trust that He cares enough about you to make sure you're covered.

YOU WON'T GIVE UP

Be joyful in hope, patient in affliction, faithful in prayer.
ROMANS 12:12 NIV

All Belinda ever wanted to do was sing. She practiced and practiced, all throughout her youth. She watched as her sisters, her friends, and her school peers auditioned for choirs, productions, and ensembles. . . and did well. She never made it. Not ever. But she refused to give up.

When she got to high school, Belinda's mom paid for her to have voice lessons. The teacher—God bless her—saw a spark of potential in young Belinda, so she worked with her on tone, pitch, and enunciation. Little by little, the voice improved. Belinda wasn't a natural, so she really had to work at it, but by her junior year she had landed a spot in the choir, and by her senior year was asked to sing the big solo in the Christmas concert. That served to boost her confidence. Undaunted by her years of struggling, Belinda went on to become a worship leader at a large church, where she used her vocal gift to lead others into God's presence week after week. She often reflected on her journey, on the many times she could have given up. How grateful she was to have stayed the course!

Not every "don't give up" story ends like Belinda's, of course, but many do. How will you ever know unless you try, after all? So what are you going to do with those things you've wanted to give up on? Maybe—just maybe—if you dared to persist, if you had the courage to

keep trying, you might accomplish your goals. Perhaps, if you don't, you will discover something else more fitting. The point is, you won't know unless you try.

The "don't give up" mentality serves us well in many areas of life. Relationships. Our job. School. You name it. And we can learn from the best example of all—Jesus. He came from heaven to earth because of His great love. The journey wasn't easy, and it pointed to His eventual death on the cross, but He refused to give up. When His opponents beat Him, tortured Him, He stayed the course. When they placed a heavy cross on His back and made Him walk the Via Dolorosa (Way of Sorrows), He did not hesitate. The journey was difficult, but He saw it through, all the way to the end. In doing so, He won the victory. . .for us!

So, what victories are yet to be won, woman of purpose? What seems too hard? Pray, and ask the Lord to give you clear direction and then all of the tenacity you need to see it through. You will make it, if you don't give up.

YOU KNOW HOW TO REST

For all who have entered into God's rest have rested from
their labors, just as God did after creating the world.
HEBREWS 4:10 NLT

Some people are just born with a strong work ethic. They come out of the womb, roll up their sleeves, and say, "Let's get to it!" They bounce from project to project with more energy than three or four other people put together.

Maybe you're one of those gals. Maybe you thrive on go, go, going. If so, you're certainly not alone. Take the story of Kendra. Talk about a worker bee! In high school, she was the president of her junior class, the year book coordinator, science lab assistant, and every other job imaginable. She even signed on as codirector of the senior play. In college she took a leadership position in her sorority and found herself immersed in excessive classes and study habits due to her double major. When she married in her late twenties, she quickly found herself frustrated with her laid-back hubby, who enjoyed his days off and didn't particularly like spending them working around the house. Kendra always had a list of things to be done and couldn't figure out why he refused to stay on task.

Kendra signed up as a volunteer at her church and eventually found herself in charge of the women's ministry. She also agreed to serve as room mother at her daughter's school and then signed up to bring snacks to her son's baseball team. Because she had experience

with drama, the local theater came calling, and before long, she was directing a play. Then two. Then three. Folks at church got wind of this and asked her to direct the Christmas play. Finally, after three years into the Christmas season, she cratered. Fell apart. Exhaustion forced her to stop completely and take a Sabbath rest.

Can you relate to Kendra? She worked, worked, worked herself into exhaustion. Her body couldn't keep up with the heavy workload, and she eventually suffered the consequences in her health and her mental state. Her marriage even suffered, as you might imagine.

There's nothing wrong with working. It's a good thing, in fact. But overworking? Risking your health? Not a good idea. God has a solution, of course. It's wrapped up in one little word: *Sabbath* (rest). Did you ever think about the fact that God initiated the Sabbath (a day of rest) for our own good? Our bodies weren't meant to go around the clock. When we push the envelope, we often pay a heavy price. So, rest, sweet sister. Rest. Do what you need to do, then say no to the rest. Come home, put your feet up, and chill. There! Doesn't that feel nice? In fact, you might just get used to it.

YOUR HEART BEATS WITH HIS

I will give you a new heart and put a new spirit in you;
I will remove from you your heart of stone
and give you a heart of flesh.

 EZEKIEL 36:26 NIV

If you've ever experienced a sense of panic, you surely know what a racing heart feels like. It's out of sync, sped up to a frightening pace. You long for your heart to beat in normal, steady time once more, for everything around you to return to normal so that your heart will be in good working order again. You long for everything to be in sync.

The same is true of staying in sync with God. When your heart is beating with His, when you're listening to His voice and staying in His Word, you don't need to panic. No racing heart. No breathless "Will I make it through this?" Instead, you can be steady. Strong. You can return to a place of safety where, day in and day out, His heartbeat and yours are one.

How does this play out in the real world? Ask Gina. For years she walked close to the Lord, trusting Him with every decision, seeking Him for every life change, praising Him, even in the bad times. Then the unthinkable happened. Gina's spouse died very suddenly, leaving her reeling. Walking in a fog. Struggling with disbelief.

For months, she questioned God. She didn't spend as much time in the Word or in prayer. She developed a "what's the point?" attitude.

In short, she got discouraged and lost track of what was once a "tight" relationship with her heavenly Father. Distrust set in. Before long, her heartbeat was completely out of sync with His. She often got that panicked feeling and wondered if things would ever get back to normal. The Lord continued to woo until she finally—bit by bit—came to trust again. Trust propelled her into His arms, where she found the healing she needed.

Maybe your story is a bit like Gina's. Some major life-shift has caused your heart to race. You wonder if it will ever slow down, ever beat in sync with the Lord's again. There's truly only one place to have the kind of heart procedure you need, sweet friend, and that's in the arms of Jesus. He's the Creator of your heart and knows exactly what it's going to take to bring it back into alignment with His. You will have to take your pain, your burdens, your grief to Him. He longs for you to bring it—and any other struggles you're going through—so that you can be healed.

An "out of sync" season can be just that. . .a season. When you run to Him, when you place your struggles at His feet, He can mend even the most broken heart.

YOUR TOUCH HEALS WOUNDS

The Spirit of the Sovereign LORD is on me, because the LORD has anointed me to proclaim good news to the poor. He has sent me to bind up the brokenhearted, to proclaim freedom for the captives and release from darkness for the prisoners.

ISAIAH 61:1 NIV

Perhaps, as a small child, you dreamed of becoming a doctor or nurse. Maybe you accomplished that goal and work in the medical field, or even on the mission field. Most of us, however, don't have the opportunity to work one-on-one with patients, to heal wounds, or to care for those in physical pain. But that doesn't mean we can't make a difference. Take a close look at today's scripture. Jesus was the ultimate example of healer. With one touch, bodies were miraculously healed, blind eyes opened, and mental anguish stilled. Does He still work like that today? Does He use us to accomplish healing?

Consider the story of Meg. She watched as a good friend, Jody, went through a tough surgery to repair a shattered ankle. Jody happened to be going through a marital breakup at the very same time and was in low spirits. Meg wondered what she could do to help. After leaving the hospital, Jody needed a place to stay, someone to care for her. Meg stepped up to the plate and opened her home, even giving up her master bedroom to her new houseguest.

During the week that Jody stayed in her home, Meg fed her, cared

for her, prayed with her, and (most of all) encouraged her. At the end of the week Jody returned to her own home, happier, healthier, and feeling better about life than she had in a long time.

Meg's role in Jody's life might seem small, but it made a huge difference to Jody. And that's the point, isn't it? We can't tend to the needs of everyone in pain, but we can make a big difference to one or two. Or three or four. Who knows how far your reach might extend if you offer yourself. And you don't just have to reach out to those in physical pain. All around you, people are hurting. Hearts are broken. Spirits are wounded. People are looking for someone to wrap their arms around them and whisper a quiet, "It's going to be okay."

Will you be that someone to a friend today? Will you heal the brokenhearted? Follow the example of our Savior, who laid down His life for us so that we could experience healing and wholeness. Be a life changer for a friend or loved one in need. In doing so, both lives will be touched and changed, and healing might just come to your heart, as well as to the other person.

YOU'VE GOT POTENTIAL

Then the way you live will always honor and please
the Lord, and your lives will produce every kind of
good fruit. All the while, you will grow as you
learn to know God better and better.

COLOSSIANS 1:10 NLT

Potential. What an interesting word. We don't always care to hear the "you've got potential" line (because it means we're not quite there yet), but folks who say it aren't just pacifying us. They really mean it. If we put our minds to it, if we apply ourselves, we'll get better at whatever we hope to do.

How does this play out in the real world? Imagine you're the parent of a child who's auditioning at a local theater. Your son preps for the audition and does his best to memorize the lines. He goes into the audition room with the directors and returns with a somber look on his face. You're concerned that he didn't do as well as he'd hoped.

Jump ahead a few days. The cast list is posted and your son is listed in the chorus. He didn't get a lead role or any sort of speaking part at all. You're convinced the director made a mistake, so you ask her about it. She responds with those words that none of us like to hear: "We really enjoyed his audition. He's got a lot of potential." Then she tells you about all of the upcoming plays they will be doing over the next couple years and says, "Maybe he'll land a speaking role, if he sticks with it."

Potential points to a future readiness, a "not quite there yet; maybe someday" response. Think about that for a moment. Likely you've got all sorts of ideas and plans for the future, but you're not quite ready to achieve your goals just yet. Maybe you want to run a marathon but can barely make it around the block. You've got potential to run but need to work up to it. The same is true with your son. If he really wants to impress the director, he should take the role in the chorus, give it his all, and then develop his skills. Move up the ranks.

So, what do you do with all of this potential that's inside of you? What do you do with that burning desire to accomplish great things, especially if you're not quite ready to dive off the board just yet? Give it to God. Ask Him to multiply it. Check your motivations. Make sure you're striving for the right things and doing it all for His sake, not your own. Watch as the word *potential* is exchanged for words like *effective, powerful. . .ready!*

Stick with it. Potential is a little tiny spark, ready to be ignited!

YOU MAKE A DIFFERENCE

Know that the LORD has set apart his faithful servant for
himself; the LORD hears when I call to him.

PSALM 4:3 NIV

Laura didn't feel that she had much to offer her friends. She wasn't a
great cook, so she couldn't bring the finest casseroles to get-togethers.
She wasn't the best singer, so she couldn't join the choir at church. She
wasn't even the finest housekeeper. In fact, she had trouble keeping her
home organized at all. In short, she felt "less than" (though she would
never have said that aloud).

One thing Laura had on her side, however, was the ability to care
deeply about her friends and to lift their spirits. She loved sending
cards and notes in the mail. She enjoyed treating friends to movies and
dinner. And when a dear friend had to be hospitalized for an extended
period of time, Laura took it upon herself to sit at her friend's bedside
for days—even weeks—on end, giving the family a much-needed break.
During this season, people thanked her profusely for her sacrifice. Only
one problem—she didn't consider what she was doing a sacrifice at all.
Didn't everyone give of themselves like this? Why did people consider
such a simple act of service a gift? Was she really making a profound
difference, as they implied?

The answer is yes! Her little "act of service" was a huge deal to
her friend and her friend's family. And though she didn't think of it as

having much value, the act of "being there" was, indeed, very valuable.

Maybe you've walked a mile in Laura's shoes. You've felt inadequate, like you didn't have much to offer. Think about what a difference the simple act of sitting at a friend's sickbed made in the life of that family. There are so many ways you can bless others, even if you don't feel "exceptionally talented" in the ways that draw attention. It's better to quietly love and care for someone than to make a big splash, anyway. You honor God in your quiet diligence and bring a smile to the faces of those looking on. You're not demanding attention or asking for applause. You're simply doing what comes naturally, which is probably why it doesn't feel like a big deal to you.

Woman of purpose, take heart! Whether you consider yourself gifted or not, you do make a difference in the lives of those around you. You really do. And you can continue to do so in the years to come. Ask the Lord to show you how to bless others when they need you most. In doing so, your talents will shine brighter than any star on the Hollywood Walk of Fame!

YOU CAN TRADE IN YOUR ASHES FOR BEAUTY

He has sent me to provide for all those who grieve in Zion,
to give them crowns instead of ashes, the oil of joy instead
of tears of grief, and clothes of praise instead of a spirit of
weakness. They will be called Oaks of Righteousness, the
Plantings of the LORD, so that he might display his glory.

ISAIAH 61:3 GW

Marti had what some friends would call "a real testimony." Before
coming to Christ, Marti worked in a job at a club that compromised her
purity in a major way. Surrounded by the wrong type of people, she
got involved with a not-so-great man and ended up pregnant. She also
battled a variety of addictions. After several years, she found help at
a women's shelter. There she learned a trade and eventually gave her
heart to the Lord. What a radical change!

You would think everything in Marti's life would be rosy after this,
but she found herself struggling to fit in with the other women at her
new church, even after she married a really great Christian man and
had two more children. She couldn't quite let go of the fact that her
past was different from the other ladies. In her eyes, it was worse than
any of the others. So, instead of sharing, she kept her mouth shut and
refused to tell anyone. She did her best to look like, act like, and dress
like the other moms but secretly saw herself as different. Her view of
herself was tainted. When she looked in the mirror, she saw the "old"

Marti, not the new one. That imprint, that image, was hard to erase. She did her best to cope but secretly wondered if she would ever get past her own negative self-image.

Maybe you can relate to her dilemma. Your past wasn't great. You feel like you're "stained" with your former sins. Oh, sweet woman of purpose! God doesn't see you that way at all. Once you're His child, the former things are passed away. Those scars, those ashes? He exchanges them for something beautiful. When He looks at you, He sees a gorgeous woman, set free and filled with purpose. No stains. No sin. Nothing to remind anyone what "used to be." Your radiant beauty comes from inside and changes everything.

No looking back. No more ashes. They're long gone. From this point on, the reflection in the mirror will be a precious, holy daughter of the Most High God.

YOU ARE NEVER ALONE

Be strong and courageous. Do not be afraid or terrified
because of them, for the LORD your God goes with you;
he will never leave you nor forsake you."

DEUTERONOMY 31:6 NIV

Lydia despised the word *alone*. She did everything in her power to fill her days with people so that she would never have to sense that awful word. Why did this word bother her so much? Because, as a youngster, she had been abandoned by her father. She could still remember the day he walked out, leaving the family, and it sickened her. So she filled the hole in her heart with people. And activities. And food. And more activities. And more food. Anything and everything to keep from feeling alone. In her "aloneness" she felt lonely. Abandoned.

As she grew in her relationship with the Lord, Lydia discovered that her "aloneness" wasn't a bad thing. In fact, she grew to enjoy her quiet times without the chaotic noise and busyness. She discovered, through her time in the Word of God, that she was never truly alone, anyway, even when there were no people around. The Bible promised that the Lord would never leave her or forsake her. What an amazing promise to a woman who'd been through such pain. Coming to grips with this brought healing in so many areas, including the overeating.

What about you? Are you filling the emptiness, the void, with activities? With people? With food? Are you like Lydia, doing all you

can to avoid spending time by yourself? Do you dread your down time? If so, it might be time to take a closer look at what's driving you to feel this way. Perhaps, like Lydia, you have abandonment issues that go back to your childhood. Or maybe you're afraid of being abandoned by a spouse or child. If so, then ask God to heal your heart so that you can come to grips with the fact that being by yourself isn't the same thing as being lonely.

Maybe you've reconciled yourself to the fact that you're never truly alone and have grown to appreciate your quiet time. No matter what you've faced, the Lord isn't going anywhere. Nothing you do can cause Him to run away. Today's scripture verse is 100 percent true: God won't leave you. He won't forsake you. There's nothing you can do to make Him turn on His heels and run. So, don't fear the quiet. Don't fret over the "alone" thing any longer. Enjoy the quiet and rest close to His heart.

YOU SEEK HIM FIRST

But seek ye first the kingdom of God, and his righteousness;
and all these things shall be added unto you.

MATTHEW 6:33 KJV

You would think that seeking God first would be a natural inclination for those of us who know and love Him. After all, He has saved us, given us new life, called us His own, given us hope for the future, and set our feet on a good path. Why, then, do we seek after other things, forgetting to ask His input?

Life is so busy. We get distracted with what's right in front of us or with our wants and wishes. We seek after the things we long for without realizing that we've put "stuff" in front of good. For example, a good friend gets a new car and we're secretly wishing we could have one too, so we work extra hard to make it happen. A relative goes on a vacation and we wish we had that opportunity. Someone at our company gets a promotion and we're wound up in knots on the inside because we wish our efforts would be noticed. And so, we seek after these things. We work hard to get that car. We pour our efforts into saving for vacation. We climb, climb, climb the corporate ladder.

There's nothing wrong with aiming for things. . .or for wanting them, for that matter. But we have to keep it all in perspective. If you look at today's scripture, you see that seeking God first puts things in the right order. When we desire Him most—when we seek Him first—these

other things will be added to us. Why? Because God knows the desires of our heart. He longs to bless us but wants to do it in His way and on His timetable.

Bobbi knew this all too well. She grew up with very little and had all sorts of desires and ambitions for what she wanted as an adult. A hard worker, she set out to make her dreams come true. Her kids would have trips to amusement parks. She and her husband would take vacations. They would live in a great home and drive nice cars. Bobbi continued to work, work, work and accomplished all of these things and more. But one thing became problematic: she sought after things first and forgot to put God in His rightful place. It took several years of acquiring "stuff" before she realized what she was doing. At that point, she took inventory of her motivation and shifted gears. No more seeking after stuff. From that point on, she made a commitment to seek the Lord first and trust Him for the rest.

Whether you're like Bobbi or you're waiting and trusting God to meet your daily needs, always remember that seeking Him first—about the things you need or want—is the answer.

There is no fear in love. But perfect love drives out
fear, because fear has to do with punishment.
The one who fears is not made perfect in love.

1 JOHN 4:18 NIV

Fear. It grips us when we least expect it. There we are, curled up under the covers, trying to sleep. . .when it hits. We can't describe the feeling, but it's something akin to having a tight cord wound around the heart, squeezing, squeezing, squeezing. It convinces us that the lights are going to be shut off, the house is going to be foreclosed on, our health is going to fail. It causes us to lie awake, tossing and turning, our stomach tied up in knots as we envision one negative scenario after another. But why? Why do we give in to fear?

Whenever we face a perceived threat, fear kicks in instinctively. We want to run away, to hide under the covers until the boogieman disappears. This is basic survival at its finest, running from fear. Whenever we think a loss is coming, we panic, whether it's loss of a job, income, valuables, relationships, or whatever we care about. We jump into fight-or-flight mode when fear grips us. Sometimes we take off running; other times we're completely locked up, frozen in place.

Where does fear come from? Is it an emotion? Is it something we can control? Fear is an archenemy, and we have to see it as such. We can't cuddle it or hold it close. We can't befriend it. The enemy of our

souls is the author of fear. He knows just how to use it against us. . .and when. Think of him in much the same way you would envision Cupid with his bow. The enemy takes aim when we are most vulnerable—during a life change, a trial, a rough patch—and slings his arrow straight at our heart. When it penetrates, that gripping sensation begins.

There's really only one way to get rid of fear. We have to replace it with trust. The Word of God is filled with hundreds of promises to convince us that the Lord is trustworthy. With God on our side, we don't have to be afraid, even if we're going through a deep valley. We can speak to fear and command it to leave.

Fear not. That's a command from the One who created you. How can He speak this with such assurance? Because He knows what's coming next and has already made a plan for how to get you through it. Don't be afraid, woman of purpose. The Creator of all is on your side.

YOUR NEEDS ARE MET

And my God will supply every need of yours
according to his riches in glory in Christ Jesus.
PHILIPPIANS 4:19 ESV

Have you ever opened your refrigerator, stared inside at all of the hundreds of food items, and then declared, "There's nothing to eat!" Might sound like a silly example, but that's often how it is when we forget to be grateful for what we have. We don't always remember that God is supernaturally supplying our every need. We're loaded with good things—a home to live in, a car to drive, friends to share the load, a decent job—and yet we feel like we're lacking. We want more.

More isn't really a bad thing, but when you're fixated on wishing, hoping, dreaming for more, more, more, it can drive you to be discontent, and discontentment is the enemy of peace. Truth is, God promises to meet your needs. And He does! That's not to say He won't lavish you abundantly, above all you could ask or think. He adores you and delights in bringing a smile to your face and by blessing you unexpectedly. But discontentment, grumbling, constantly striving for more, more, more. . . well, these things will distract you from where you need to be.

The next time you open your refrigerator, pause for a moment and thank God for what He has already supplied. Ask Him to give you that same sense of satisfaction about your home, your wardrobe, your job. And remember, God cares more about you than He does all of the rest

of nature. If He clothes the birds, if He tends to the animals in the field, supplying their every need. . .won't He do even more for you, His child?

God will provide. He will. We still work. We still have wants and wishes, but ultimately, every good thing comes from above. Don't believe it? Ask Andrea. She and her husband lived a simple life. Their house wasn't large. Their car often needed work. But she diligently praised God for every blessing. Every time an unexpected check came in, every time an appliance lasted longer than she expected, she praised Him. Instead of craving more, more, more, she settled the issue in her heart and expressed gratitude for what was right in front of her. As a result, the Lord gave her more. Andrea's husband got an offer of a job and they ended up moving to a new home in another city. A bigger home. Not that it really mattered to Andrea. She'd been perfectly content in the old home.

Can you relate to her story, or are you constantly striving for more? Today, why not pause and thank God for meeting your every need. If He chooses to bless you above and beyond what you need, then praise Him all over again!

YOU DELIGHT IN HIM

Take delight in the LORD, and he will give
you the desires of your heart.
PSALM 37:4 NIV

Don't you just love the word *delight*? It conjures up images of laughter, giggles, and an all-around great time. To delight means to "please greatly." When was the last time you were so pleased with the way things were going that you found yourself lighthearted and giggly? Here's a fun thought: God feels that way. . .about you! That's right! When He thinks about you, He's greatly pleased.

Okay, so you're probably wondering why He's so excited about you. You're his child! And sure, you make mistakes, but don't all kids? This doesn't stop us from loving them, does it? Our little ones still bring smiles to our faces, even when they're being naughty.

In the same way that God delights in us, we should delight in Him. The only way we can accomplish this is by sticking close to Him, by satisfying ourselves with His presence, His Word. When we're communing with Him, our "friendship level" is more intimate. When you're intimate with the Lord, you're tickled by the things that tickle Him. When He blesses a good friend with a job, you celebrate. When He touches a family member and heals them of their sickness, you are thrilled. In short, you're thrilled by all of the good things He does. And even when you're going through a rough patch, you still trust that He's looking

out for your well-being.

Think about your relationship with your children (or grandchildren or nieces or nephews). How and why do they bring you delight? Honestly, they don't have to do a thing, do they? It's not about performance. But when they sing silly songs or dance around the living room to entertain you, your heart wants to burst with pride. Why? Because they're just so happy to be with you. That's it! They are delighting in your presence, and you respond with pure pleasure that they have gone to such efforts to bless you.

Kendra understood this. Her two daughters kept her running ragged, especially during the preschool years. She would tidy up the living room, they would drag out toys. She would do their laundry, they would play in the dirt. They were kids, after all. Just about the time she felt exhausted and frazzled, one or both of them would break into a silly song from their favorite movie. In an instant, all stresses floated away on that precious melody. She forgot about her troubles and relished in the joy of simply being with them.

In the same way, we bless God's heart by sticking close to Him. In response, we are blessed by His presence. We love. . .and are loved in return. What a perfect recipe for delight!

YOU ARE PERFECTLY IMPERFECT

All of us make a lot of mistakes. If someone doesn't make
any mistakes when he speaks, he would be perfect.
He would be able to control everything he does.

JAMES 3:2 GW

Do you remember the movie *Mary Poppins*? Mary described herself
as "practically perfect in every way." Some people have more self-
confidence than others, apparently! Of course, Mary wasn't really
perfect. Not even close. No one is. Most of us aren't like Mary. We're
actually hyperfocused on our flaws. We're not bragging about our level
of perfection. In fact, we find it difficult to see our good points because
we're so focused on the bad. Maybe that's just part of being female,
but it's something we need to come to grips with. Why? Because our
perceived imperfections make us hesitate in so many areas. We hesitate to get close to others, worried about what they'll think about us.
We're even hesitant to draw near to God, afraid He will push us away
because we don't measure up. Oh, if only we could break past these
feelings of insecurity and inadequacy!

Today, instead of worrying about all of the things you find wrong
with yourself—the extra pounds, the wrinkles, the inabilities, the mistakes
you've made—why not thank God for your imperfections? If you were
perfect, you wouldn't need Him. Your beautiful imperfections offer Him
the opportunity to shine through. When you feel ugly, He stirs up the

beauty on the inside and adds a sparkle to your eyes that makes you gorgeous to others. When you struggle with inadequacy, He takes up the slack. When you take a tumble, He's there to brush off the dust and put you on your feet again.

There's only One who has achieved perfection, and that's your Creator. He knows that you're flawed. He's not shocked by your imperfections. But, neither does He want you to rehearse them. Why? Because you're created in His image. Can you imagine if one of your children went on and on and on about how flawed they felt? It would break your heart. In the same way that a parent would comfort a child and whisper, "You're pure perfection to me!" our heavenly Father leans down and whispers in our ear, "You're more than enough for me! Stop worrying about not being worthy. Stop worrying about having to prove yourself to Me. Just relax. Be yourself. I'll take care of the rest. In fact, I already have. . .on Calvary."

Wow! If we saw our imperfections through the lens of the cross, it would change everything. No longer would we feel that we had anything to prove. Instead, we could simply live our lives, free to love the Lord and receive His love in response.

Look past your insecurities, woman of purpose. Give them to God. It won't be long before you're celebrating your perfectly perfect imperfections.

YOU ARE MOTIVATED BY JOY

I have told you this so that my joy may be
in you and that your joy may be complete.
JOHN 15:11 NIV

Have you ever met one of those women who just radiated joy? Her bubbly personality trickled over into every area of life? Maybe you are that woman. Perhaps people are drawn to you because of your positive, upbeat spin on things.

Joyful women are so much fun to be around. They're not zeroing in on the problems, they're rejoicing over the solutions, even before the solutions come. They speak in faith, live in faith, and make decisions with faith. That's why they're free to experience such joy, because they haven't put their trust in themselves. They've settled the "God's got this" issue.

Some people think they can "try harder" to be happy, but here's the truth: you can't produce joy. There's no magic formula or recipe for a joyous life. Really, the only thing you can do is release your hold on the things you weren't meant to control and give them to God. Once you've let go, you're free! You're content. You're not striving anymore. Instead, you're flourishing. In a sense, it's like losing a lot of weight. . .all at once. There's something about being a lightweight that brings great joy.

Of course, not all women—even Christian women—have figured out the joy thing. Take Missy, for instance. She had a tendency to see the glass as half empty, not half full. Sure, she had a relationship with the

Lord. She attended church every Sunday, even taught Sunday school in the children's department. But, try as she may, she just couldn't seem to keep a positive attitude or disposition. When someone would ask, "How are you doing, Missy?" she would respond with a laundry list of things that had gone wrong that week. On and on she would go, describing every negative thing in great detail. In short, she was a downer. A real downer.

No one actually came out and told Missy that they were turned off by her negativity, but one by one, people stopped engaging her in conversation. She noticed that the few people who still connected with her always seemed to change the conversation when she would start describing her woes. Before long, she got it. A good friend challenged her to a "Keep It Positive for Thirty Days" challenge, and she took the hint. Before long, her attitude slowly morphed into something more upbeat. As a result of this attitude shift, joy filled her heart. Missy changed, from the inside out. No, her situation didn't change, but she learned to experience joy, even in the middle of life's daily dramas and traumas.

You don't have to have a perfect life to be filled with joy, my friend. All it takes is a change in perspective.

YOU ARE ON A LEARNING CURVE

I pray that your love will overflow more and more, and that
you will keep on growing in knowledge and understanding.
PHILIPPIANS 1:9 NLT

Some people are such know-it-alls! You can't tell them anything without hearing the words, "Well, actually. . ." followed by a lengthy story about how they can do it better, grander, smarter, etc. You can't teach them anything. That's a shame, because no one really knows it all. Even the most educated person you know probably has days where they don't know what to do. Let's face it. . .we're all on a learning curve, no matter how many years of experience or training we have under our belts.

God's not keen on watching His daughters, even those with purpose-filled lives, coming across as puffed-up know-it-alls. It's better to admit you're still on a learning curve. This takes humility, for sure, but humbling yourself is always more attractive to those who are watching you. And there are people watching you, you know. They're waiting for those "I'm so perfect" gals to slip up. And slip up, they do! Just one more reason why you shouldn't present an infallible image. When you tumble, everyone will notice.

Here's an example: Maybe you've been put in charge of a big project at work because you've made it clear you've got the goods. The boss is convinced you've got the goods and places you over a team of co-workers. Things go well. . .at first. Then, somewhere along the way you

hit the wall and don't know what to do. The team gets nervous, but more than that, they start talking behind your back. Why? Because you were overly confident and they've been waiting all along to see you take a tumble. It's just human nature.

What do you do in a situation like this? It's time to turn to God and admit that you don't have all the answers. You're not superwoman. You're still on a learning curve. And guess what? You've given your heart to the One who has all the answers to your questions. He's the ultimate professor, fully equipped with answers from on high. Somewhere along the way, you also need to humble yourself in front of your peers and make some apologies. Let them know that you're not perfect. Not even close. When you get real with them, they're more likely to lend true support and to help you get the job done in a pleasant environment.

Being on a learning curve is nothing to be ashamed of. All of life is a "schooling" experience, after all. So buckle your seat belt, students! It might get a little rocky in here!

YOU REJOICE IN TRIBULATION

Be joyful in hope, patient in affliction, faithful in prayer.
ROMANS 12:12 NIV

Have you ever examined the word *tribulation*? On the surface, it seems like a happy-go-lucky word. Four syllables that roll off the tongue with ease. Unfortunately, tribulation isn't easy. It doesn't just "roll off." It's a season of trial and testing that sometimes goes on and on. We all go through seasons of tribulation, but knowing how to come out on the other side with a smile on our face. . .that's not so easy. Still, it is possible.

Constance knew what it was like to go through tribulation. It seemed she always walked through it, one episode after another. She often wondered if she would ever have a normal life or if chaos would always rule the day. When she was newly married, her husband lost his job. Then, during her pregnancy with their third daughter, Constance got really ill and had to be hospitalized. The baby was born under emergency circumstances. All of this cost money they didn't have. Their daughter was born with medical issues, and Constance spent years going back and forth to doctors, pediatricians, and specialists. This also impacted her daughter's ability to attend school, so Constance ended up homeschooling, something she'd never dreamed she would do. Her daughter grew into a young woman but had a lot of health struggles along the way.

You would think that all this tribulation would wear on Constance,

that she would spend her days doubting God and complaining about her situation. Just the opposite was true! Friends took note of her positive disposition, even in the middle of the trials. In the midst of great affliction and suffering, her endurance, her patience, her positive, upbeat spin on things, served as the most amazing testimony of God's grace.

Her friends and loved ones learned a lot by watching her go through such a fiery season. She learned a lot too—like how to come out of a fire without so much as the smell of smoke in her hair. Funny. When you praise your way through a storm, you hardly remember going through it at all.

Maybe you're in the midst of a storm right now. Maybe tribulation has the best of you. You don't feel like rejoicing. If you want to come through it all unscathed, here's the best advice of all: Don't give in to the temptation to let your disposition sour. Instead, lift that voice in praise. Doing so will change your perspective and will flood your soul with joy, unspeakable joy! And maybe—just maybe—your upbeat reaction to life's challenges will serve as a witness to someone else. What an amazing testimony that will be.

YOUR LIFE IS A REMARKABLE STORY

Let the redeemed of the LORD tell their story—
those he redeemed from the hand of the foe.
PSALM 107:2 NIV

Have you ever wished you could write a book or a movie? If you could, what sort of story would you design? Would the hero and heroine meet in an unexpected way? Would they fall in love? Would there be action and adventure? Stories are a lot of fun to read (and watch on TV or in movies), but the greatest, most amazing story of all is the one God is writing right now—the story of your life. It's got amazing plot twists, loaded with ups and downs in all the right places. And talk about characterization! God has loaded your story with amazing characters and subcharacters, sure to keep the pages turning. Sure, you don't know what's coming in the next chapter, but that's part of the fun! God, the Author of your story, is the best writer of all.

Aubrey wasn't so sure she could trust God with her story. In fact, she had a hard time letting go of the reins at all. Some people would call her a control freak. Aubrey would just say that she liked things the way she liked them. From the time she was a little girl, Aubrey had a plan for her life. She knew what she wanted to be when she grew up (an architect, like her dad). She knew where she wanted to go to college. Nothing in Aubrey's story turned out the way she wanted. After her father passed away, Aubrey's mother didn't end up having the money

to send her to college, so she went to a local junior college instead. She took her basics but was never able to move on from there to a university, so the architecture degree was nothing more than a fleeting fancy. At some point she took a job at a local EMS call center. From there, the strange and unfamiliar desire to become a paramedic took hold. She couldn't believe it. Hadn't she always wanted to be an architect?

And yet. . .the nagging sense that she should become a paramedic wouldn't leave her alone. So, she trained to do just that and ended up working on an ambulance. The job fulfilled her and left her wondering how or why she'd ever wanted anything else.

Aubrey learned the hard way that letting go—though hard—was the only way to truly get beyond her own wants and get to where God wanted her to be. Her story was filled with twists and turns (and she never would've guessed the plotline as a youngster) but in the end, she had to admit that God was a far greater writer than she was.

The Lord has a wonderful plan for your happily-ever-after, one that dates back to the work that Jesus did on the cross. So you know you can trust Him, woman of purpose. Your story will end well.

YOU CAN FINISH WELL

However, I consider my life worth nothing to me;
my only aim is to finish the race and complete
the task the Lord Jesus has given me—the task
of testifying to the good news of God's grace.

ACTS 20:24 NIV

Have you ever started a diet, only to quit a few days or weeks later? Have you ever joined a gym and gone faithfully. . .for a month or two? Have you ever made up your mind to keep your house organized, only to find it in a state of chaos a short time later? If so, then join the crowd! Women—even women with a great sense of purpose—are often great starters but poor finishers.

Take Angela, for instance. She was a great starter. Over the years, she started hundreds of scrapbooking projects. She started new jobs. Started painting rooms in her house. Started new hobbies, like quilting. She even started a book, convinced she wanted to be a writer. Problem was, Angela never seemed to finish much. She couldn't quite go the distance with her projects or (ultimately) her relationships. For some reason, she always gave up before getting to the finish line.

Are you a great starter? Do you dive in, loaded with energy? What happens next? Does your excitement wane? Do things peter out? If you're like Angela, then there's a phrase you might want to write down and keep on your bathroom mirror: "I want to be a woman who finishes well."

Life is a race. We start off at the crack of the pistol and tear out of the gate. But sooner or later, we're bound to get tired. Distracted. That's the most critical leg of the race because it determines whether or not we will continue. It's not how we start that matters, after all. It's how we finish. And we won't finish at all if we give up too soon. Sure, we won't always make it to our goal weight, but we can keep going, even when it's tough. Especially when it's tough. And true, we won't always have a perfectly organized home, but that shouldn't stop us from an ongoing attempt to keep things orderly and neat.

What areas of your life are the most out of balance? Ask the Lord to give you a plan—one you can keep for years to come. Then, slowly, carefully, take your first step. Don't try to do everything at once. Small steps are still steps. Progress is progress. You will be more likely to finish well if you start slowly, strategically. Remember, it's not how you start. . .it's how you finish. And you, woman of purpose, can finish very, very well, if you don't give up.

YOU ARE A WOMAN OF GRACE

But to each one of us grace has been
given as Christ apportioned it.
EPHESIANS 4:7 NIV

Women are funny creatures. They hear one word and think of another. For instance, many hear the word *grace* and think it means "graceful." They shrug it off and say, "Well, that's not me." Interestingly enough, grace isn't about our ability to move gracefully at all—not physically, anyway. It's about our ability to live our lives in a gracious, merciful way.

Maybe you've seen the word broken down this way: G.R.A.C.E.— God's Riches at Christ's Expense. To be filled with grace means that we've accepted the Lord's free gift, and at no cost to us. We're blessed, even when we don't deserve it.

Imagine you've been given a huge monetary gift—a million dollars. You've done nothing to deserve it. You don't even really know your benefactor, though you want to get to know him once he's given the gift. You're overwhelmed by the extreme generosity and goodness of this stranger and feel the need to somehow repay him, but he won't accept anything from you. All he wants—he says—is for you to stop by his house every now and again for a cup of coffee and a chat. And so you oblige. You're more than happy to spend time with the one who cared enough to bless you.

Understanding God's grace is a bit like that. We can't comprehend

why the God of the universe would choose to reach down and bestow His unmerited favor on us, flawed as we are. And yet, He did. He freely offered all that He had so that we could enter into relationship with Him, and also so that we would have all we need in this life, not just to survive, but to thrive.

God's riches at Christ's expense. All of this wondrous blessing, lavished on us, but someone had to pay the price. Jesus, God's only Son, gave His life on Calvary so that we could have it all. But it doesn't stop there. That same grace flows out of us toward others that we spend time with. In the same way that God freely bestowed, we need to freely bestow. How does that play out? When someone cuts you off in traffic, extend grace. When someone at work loses his or her temper, you grace them through it. You're willing to extend grace because you've received it in such abundance.

Ah, grace. It truly is amazing, isn't it? A woman of purpose recognizes this and is grateful for it.

YOUR LIGHT SHINES BRIGHT

In the same way, let your light shine before others, that they
may see your good deeds and glorify your Father in heaven.
MATTHEW 5:16 NIV

Imagine you're on a ship in the middle of the night. The sea is dark. The skies are black. The ocean is calm and quiet. You trust the captain's navigational skills, but something about the process seems a bit eerie. Seeing around the next bend would make you more comfortable, wouldn't it? Crawling through the murky waters in the pitch black is downright terrifying. Now picture a lighthouse a few miles off in the distance. Its light—a beacon in the night—flashes, offering hope. Comfort.

Think about the many people you know who are drifting out to sea (spiritually speaking), enveloped by darkness. They are lost in the murky blackness of night. Then, suddenly, they see you—a lighthouse. You are a beacon, offering hope, joy, peace. You radiate God's brilliant light, offering them a chance to see beyond their circumstances, through the murky darkness and into a hopeful future. Light is an amazing thing. Just one light shimmers, and hope springs up.

Leigh wasn't sure she could be a light in the darkness because she stumbled so often. As a teen she bounced back and forth between good and bad. Half the time she was the sweet church girl, active in the youth group. The other half of the time she got caught up in the party scene at school and did some things she regretted. As much as she wanted to

let her light shine while with her school friends, she seemed to fall short.

It wasn't until Leigh graduated from college that she got serious about her relationship with the Lord. By then, it was too late to undo the damage that had been done early on, but at least she reached a point where she cared about her witness, her testimony. Before long, she truly became a light in the darkness, one that drew people to the Lord. Before that could happen, however, she had to forgive herself for the many times she'd let her light go out. Oh, how she wished she could go back in time and undo some not-so-great things.

What about you? Is your little light shining so that others can come to know the Lord? Today, spend some time in prayer and ask the Lord to show you how you can better radiate His brilliant light so that others are drawn to Him. What are you waiting for, woman of purpose? Let that little light shine!

YOU ARE A WORLD CHANGER

With all your heart you must trust the LORD and not
your own judgment. Always let him lead you,
and he will clear the road for you to follow.

PROVERBS 3:5–6 CEV

As a young woman, Heather dreamed of changing the world. She went on her first missions trip at age eighteen and was thrilled—albeit terrified—to work with a team that smuggled Bibles into the (then-Communist) Soviet Union. Talk about scary! She risked her life to spread the Gospel, and the sense of gratification that came with such an adventure made her feel satisfied. Every day was filled with an overwhelming sense of making a difference in the lives of people she came in contact with. Talk about gratifying!

Jump ahead several years. Heather married and had two children in three years. She found herself in a completely different sort of life. Diapers. Bottles. Pediatricians. Dirty dishes in the sink. Laundry piled up in the basket. Babies crying in the wee hours of the night. Gone were the days of heart-racing adventure, replaced with a new life that (frankly) felt mundane at times. She adored her family but sometimes wondered if she would ever get back to the business of reaching others for Christ. Were those days behind her?

Maybe you can relate to Heather's story. Maybe you once dreamed of making a difference in the world and you're at the "is my time behind

me?" point. Here's the truth: Heather's "adventure" with her husband and children was just as magnificent in God's eyes as her frightening escapades smuggling Bibles underground. Maybe more so. For, in raising her children, she had the opportunity to transform their lives on a daily basis. To walk with them in the way. To pour into their lives as no one else could.

Take a look at today's scripture. If we're really trusting God with our whole hearts, if we're leaning on Him for every decision, then we have to believe that He's leading and guiding us at every given moment. He's clearing the road. Sure, that road might look different than we'd imagined, but if it's His road, it's the right road. There's no safer—or more effective—place to be than the center of the Lord's perfect will.

Sometimes we don't have to look beyond our own window to find the place God wants us to be. And the "difference" we make in the lives of our children, neighbors, friends, and coworkers can be substantial. Sure, many are called across the globe to preach the Gospel, and perhaps you're one of them. But while you're waiting—if you're waiting—don't despise the small things. Or, rather, don't despise the things that look small. They are, indeed, quite large.

The sweet smell of incense can make you feel good,
but true friendship is better still.
PROVERBS 27:9 CEV

Brianna loved her friends and would do just about anything for them. They all knew they could count on her. Some counted on her more than others, to the point of taking advantage of her. One friend, in particular, intruded on Brianna's good nature and on her time. Tina had a lot of issues. Financial. Emotional. Relational. She leaned on Brianna for support and ended up asking for a loan. Then she needed a place to stay. She agreed to help share the utility bills but never could come up with the money. Brianna let her stay. . .too long. When she finally spoke up, Tina got angry and moved on, taking advantage of another susceptible friend.

Maybe you're like Brianna. You love your friends and would do just about anything for them. You've followed the "lay down your life for your friends" scripture to a T. Sometimes this approach has worn you out and you've been taken advantage of. Be careful! Your excessive generosity could very well lead to an unhealthy relationship, and before long, you might just find that your so-called "friend" has drained you dry! Some seemingly healthy friendships can turn on a dime and become codependent nightmares!

God wants us to be a good friend, but He's not keen on people taking advantage of us. Sometimes the best sort of friend is the one

who speaks truth (in love) to the other, even when it's hard. Especially when it's hard. If you're involved with someone who's draining you, this might be the time to speak up, before things get even stickier!

Perhaps it's time to assess your friendships, woman of purpose. You might need to make a list with all of your closest friends' and acquaintances' names on it. Divide it into columns and do an honest assessment. Take a look at who's encouraging you and who's draining you. Godly relationships are based on love, true, but they're also based on Jesus' teachings. He didn't drain His friends. He encouraged them, loved them, taught them, built them up. Go to the Lord with your list and ask His opinion. Be honest with Him about how you feel. He will show you who to keep on the list and who to gently nudge to the side. Sometimes we have to do that, you know. . .ease our way out of relationships that aren't healthy.

Jesus loved others, but He loved the Father more. When you're walking in close relationship with your heavenly Father, you'll have the insight and wisdom necessary to make the right decisions. So, be a friend, but keep those friendships in balance.

YOU'VE LAID DOWN YOUR GRUMBLING

Do all things without grumbling or disputing.
PHILIPPIANS 2:14 ESV

Grumbling. We don't mean to do it. But there it is. . .a gripe. A complaint. A snide comment. It slips out without so much as a moment's thought. And with it comes a wee bit of attitude, a rush of emotion, and the feeling that, perhaps, no one on earth has things as bad as we do.

What's wrong with grumbling? It affects our thoughts, and our thoughts affect our heart, our relationships, and our potential. How does it affect our potential, you ask? When we're whining about things that haven't even happened yet, we're speaking negatively over them. Any sense of excitement or adventure about it gets zapped in the negative emotions. So, in essence, it's removing our "potential" for something good to happen and replacing it with a "glass is half empty" mind-set.

Katrina didn't mean to grumble. In fact, she didn't even realize that's what she was doing. But day in and day out, she nit-picked over problems. If she didn't like something, she spoke up, even if it meant hurting feelings. She griped about her daughter's messy hair, her husband's unwillingness to put his dirty socks in the hamper, her boss's penchant for tardiness. On and on she went, finding fault with a thousand things, always willing to draw attention to them. Like a broken record, she spouted the same old things, over and over again, rarely pointing out the positive, and always hyper-focusing on the negative.

Are you like Katrina? Do the "little" things that others do bug you? Do you feel like you have to comment? Here's an idea, woman of purpose! Give yourself a window of time—maybe thirty days—where you make up your mind not to grumble. Ask a family member or good friend to hold you accountable. Maybe she can give you some sort of code word to stop you in your tracks. And while you're at it, why not replace your grumbles with words of praise? Instead of griping at that family member who can't seem to get his or her clothes in the laundry basket, why not offer some sort of incentive? Come up with a fun plan. Make it a game.

When you let go of grumbling, you're a lot more fun to be around. And the person who gets the most benefit? It's you, of course! Grumbling ties us up in knots, and what woman needs that? So make up your mind to see the glass as half full, not half empty. You'll be shocked at how this change of perspective changes the words that come out of your mouth!

YOU ARE GOING PLACES

Practice these things, immerse yourself in them,
so that all may see your progress.
1 TIMOTHY 4:15 ESV

Imagine you're headed out on an extended road trip across multiple states. You would surely pack for the journey and make sure you had plenty of gas in the car. You would plan ahead for each day's travel and would make reservations at hotels along the way. You might even plan to stop at amusement parks or your favorite restaurants. What fun, knowing you've got the open road ahead of you and so much to look at and do along the way. Talk about an adventure! And how wonderful to have it carefully planned out. You feel safe with a plan in motion.

Life is a journey, much like a road trip. There are so many exciting stops along the way—some planned and others unexpected. And God has specific destinations in mind. Sure, the ultimate destination is heaven, but think of all the places He wants to take you in this life! What an adventure!

Of course, our plans don't always pan out like we think. Take Barbara's journey, for instance. Barbara was a lover of life. She mapped out her life journey in much the same way she mapped out her road trips with the family. Every detail got penciled in on a spreadsheet. Talk about details! Barbara knew just what would happen. . . and when. Then, about twenty years into her marriage, her husband

was diagnosed with prostate cancer. Everything changed in a day. She couldn't put anything on a spreadsheet anymore. No longer could she map out her days. Everything became a big blur. She wondered if things would ever get back to normal. Her husband underwent treatment and eventually recovered, but Barbara's penchant for writing things down waned a bit. Why try to control it all when it wasn't hers to control in the first place?

Maybe you're a bit like Barbara. You're a planner. Your journey has had its ups and downs, ins and outs, and you're at a fork in the road. Maybe you wonder which way to turn. Or, worse. . .maybe you think you're out of options. Take heart, woman of purpose! Your journey isn't over. There's such a bright road ahead of you. Sure, you've already traveled to great places (spiritually, relationally, etc.) in your life, but there's plenty of road ahead. Adventures await! Maybe you can't map out what's coming next, but that's where faith kicks in. What fun would it be, to always have the reins in hand? Let God take control, then watch as He leads you down unexpected roads, filled with life lessons and precious blessings.

YOU RELISH IN THE QUIET

"Be still, and know that I am God. I will be exalted
among the nations, I will be exalted in the earth!"
PSALM 46:10 ESV

Quiet. There's so little of it in today's society. TVs blare, radios make us tap
our toes, kids holler at each other. Horns honk, tires squeal, construction
vehicles drive you mad with their noise. All around us life hums, hums,
hums. . .and often at a frantic level. Rarely do we have the opportunity
just to sit in total silence and ponder the deeper things of life.

Jenny understood this. She decided to take a much-needed weekend
away at a retreat center with her friends. Getting away from the hustle
and bustle worked wonders! Once there, she found time to walk the
trails in the woods and spend a lot of time in total peace and quiet. It
took awhile to adjust, but she finally settled in and enjoyed being away
from the chaos.

Patricia found another way to celebrate silence. She attended a
retreat center run by nuns where participants/guests were expected
to observe a state of total silence during their time there. She found it
difficult (what woman wouldn't?), but the whole experience ended up
being very therapeutic and cleansing. Only in the silence could she truly
hear God's voice. Only in the silence could she deal with the emotions
and thoughts she'd been struggling with.

Sometimes we really do need to retreat. It's not bad to get away.

Even Jesus did it, when He retreated to the garden of Gethsemane on the night He was betrayed. In that quiet place He poured out His heart to the Father and received the comfort He needed for the gruesome journey ahead. We can learn from His example. Getting away, if only for a few hours or days, can make all the difference because it gives us an opportunity to truly communicate with God in a more intimate way.

If you could go away to a quiet place for a day or two, where would you go? Would you draw near to the Lord in the silence? Perhaps it's time to put together a plan of action. Choose a place. If you truly can't get away, then take an hour or two to walk the trails in your neighborhood or a nearby park. Being out in nature is so helpful because you're surrounded by the beauty of creation, which always makes you more mindful of God's presence.

However you "get away," do so with this motivation: God wants to speak to you in the silence. He will, you know. So keep your ears open. Beyond the sound of the birds tweeting and the crickets chirping, you might just hear a little whisper from heaven.

But those who obey God's word truly show how completely
they love him. That is how we know we are living in him.

1 JOHN 2:5 NLT

You know that feeling you get after eating a wonderful dinner? You
feel satisfied. Full. Happy. Content. You're not opening the pantry door,
wondering what else you can find to eat. You've had the very thing you
wanted and it satisfied you. In fact, it brought so much fulfillment that
you wonder if you can get up off the sofa for the rest of the evening!

That same sense of satisfaction and fulfillment can be yours every
day as you walk with Christ. You don't have to hunger and thirst after
other things. No distractions. Nothing else looks appealing but your
relationship with God. Why even go there? You don't want to try anything
else because you already know it'll leave you feeling empty.

Natalie understood the word *empty*. She felt that way growing up.
A latchkey kid, she came home to an empty house every day. Her mom
would rush in after a long day and toss some fast food Natalie's way,
then buzz off to her computer to wrap up whatever work she hadn't
finished at the office. With no father in the picture and no siblings to
bring comfort, Natalie felt pretty empty and alone.

When she reached her teens, she went in search of something to
fill that emptiness. Relationships with boys? She had plenty. Bouncing
from one to the other convinced her that the answer wasn't found there,

but she didn't mind trying again. And again. And again. It wasn't until Natalie went to college that things began to change. She was invited to a Bible study and decided to give it a try. That choice changed everything. Once there, she settled into the group, received the love she needed from the others in the group, and eventually gave her heart to the Lord. The emptiness was no longer an issue once her heart was filled with God's peace and with the love of her friends.

Think of a time in your life when you felt empty. Not a very pleasant feeling, is it? It's more dangerous than driving your car on "E" but similar in many ways. When your car is out of gas, it sits in the garage, unusable. When you reach the empty point in your spiritual life, you sit in a quiet, lonely place, wondering if you have any purpose at all. You do, sweet sister! You are loaded with purpose, and God wants that sense of fulfillment to drive and motivate you. Don't look for other things to fill the void. Turn to Him, and ask for a "fill up" today. Then watch as He satisfies you from the inside out.

YOU ARE A REFLECTION OF CHRIST

The Son is the radiance of God's glory and the exact
representation of his being, sustaining all things by his
powerful word. After he had provided purification for sins,
he sat down at the right hand of the Majesty in heaven.

HEBREWS 1:3 NIV

Oh, the dreaded mirror! Most women have a love/hate relationship with it. On a good day, the mirror serves as friend and encourager. On a bad day (or during a rough season) it's the worst enemy in the world. In it, we see the things we wish we didn't have to see—the flaws, the imperfections. When we close our eyes, we can envision ourselves differently, but in the mirror, we're faced with the obvious, undeniable truth, and it's not always what we'd hoped.

Bridget learned this the hard way. During her younger years she was the picture of perfection. Perfect figure. Lovely face. Beautiful features. She had everything going for her. When she entered her twenties, she was hit hard with unexpected physical pain and a variety of unusual symptoms, including a rash on her face. By her early thirties she was diagnosed with an autoimmune disease (lupus) that affected her joints and her overall health. The image in the mirror gradually began to change as her body succumbed to the illness. Her physical beauty, though still there, seemed to fade, at least in Bridget's point of view. And this only became more complicated when the doctor put her on daily steroids,

which caused her face to look puffy. Would she ever be normal again, or would the reflection in the mirror continue to haunt her?

It took some time (and the help of loving friends and family members), but Bridget finally came to grips with the face in the mirror. She learned that her "reflection" wasn't what she saw in the mirror at all. Instead, she was a reflection of Jesus Christ, who adored her and wanted His best for her. Instead of focusing on what she couldn't change outwardly, she went to work on the inward changes, the heart changes. Before long, she was at peace, from the inside out. And that, of course, showed up in the reflection in the mirror. After all, there's much to be said for a peaceful, contented countenance. It can make even the plainest face lovely.

Maybe you're not happy with the image in the mirror today. Remember, you're a reflection of your heavenly Father, who wants to leave His imprint on your heart, not necessarily your face. Just something to ponder as you give yourself one last glimpse in the mirror before heading out for your day.

YOUR STRENGTH COMES FROM HIM

GOD, the Lord, is my strength; he makes my feet like the
deer's; he makes me tread on my high places.

HABAKKUK 3:19 ESV

Remember that old cartoon, *Popeye the Sailor Man*? Popeye was weak until he ate his spinach. Then. . .bam! Muscles! Internal fortitude! External abilities! Wow. Talk about the perfect solution. And it all seemed so easy.

We all need a can of spinach from time to time, don't we? Even women of purpose—strong, godly women with drive and zeal—can crater when things get out of control. Life can zap the strength right out of us, especially if we're carrying a heavy load or tending to the needs of others. Circumstances and situations can pull the proverbial plug and our energy leaks out. We feel drained. Empty. Weak. Our spiritual muscles shrivel up. That's when we need to remember Popeye. He didn't accomplish the instantaneous feats of muscle-ladened strength by himself. He relied on his source, his can of spinach. And yes, it really was just that easy. A few bites, and. . .bam! His entire perspective changed.

You rely on your source too, only it's not found in a can of spinach. Your source is your Creator. He gives you everything you need to turn your situation around. Feeling weak? Turn to His Word and watch as He brings an instantaneous change of perspective. Feeling like you can't keep going? Pray, and watch as you're imbued with strength from on high. Feeling like you've taken on too much? Toss that heavy load His

way and watch as He carries it for you, relieving you of the stress and the pressure. God is good, and His mercies go on. . .forever. He longs for you to be healthy and strong, not just because you have work to do, but because He adores you and wants the best for you.

Think of your daily time in the Word like a trip to the gym. It's not always easy at first, but after a while your muscles grow, grow, grow. You're able to handle a heavier load. Picture yourself lifting weights. You start small and then get stronger over time until you can finally lift more than you thought possible.

When you're weak, He is strong. And that strength is all you need. It takes your weakness (think atrophied muscles) and "grows" them into something capable of heavy lifting. So, no can of spinach necessary, woman of purpose! All you need is to draw close to your heavenly Father. Reach for Him. Reach for His Word. Then watch as He fills you with supernatural strength, guaranteed to see you through.

YOU ARE STRONGER THAN TEMPTATION

No temptation has overtaken you except what is common to mankind. And God is faithful; he will not let you be tempted beyond what you can bear. But when you are tempted, he will also provide a way out so that you can endure it.

1 CORINTHIANS 10:13 NIV

Temptation. Ugh! How we hate it. We're buzzing along, doing just fine, resisting, resisting, resisting, and then. . .bam. Temptation hits. We see it with our eyes and want it. We're sure we won't crater, but then we do. After the temptation comes the inevitable season of regret, where we beat ourselves up and commit to never fall off the wagon again.

Alice understood this well. With thirty pounds to lose, she put herself on a strict diet. No sugar. No dairy. No bread. Yes, this seemed a little extreme, but this time—this time—she would stay the course. She would lose the weight.

Alice pinched her eyes shut while others around her ate the things she secretly craved. Nope. She wouldn't give in. Then, a situation at work went sour. Alice was falsely accused. Badly hurt. On the way home from the office, she drove through a fast food restaurant and got a large order of french fries. And an ice cream cone. The very things she'd tried to avoid were the first things she turned to for comfort. Afterward, she felt physically (and emotionally) ill. She also felt really stupid. How could

she have done the very thing she vowed not to do? Didn't she see the consequences?

Maybe you've walked a mile in Alice's shoes. You've told yourself, "I won't do that" or "I won't eat that," only to crater. Afterward, you felt so defeated. Don't let it get you down for long, woman of purpose! Here's the truth: Temptations come and temptations go. They will always tug at us, urging us to do the wrong things. But today's scripture assures us that no temptation—no piece of chocolate cake, no relationship, no financial ploy—will overtake us if we allow God to take control. Sure, temptation has its draw, but nothing beyond what we can bear. The Lord will provide a way out, if we ask Him.

So ask Him! If you're facing a temptation right now, turn your eyes away from it. Repeat these words: "Make a better choice." With God's help, you can and will. And when you make mistakes (and you surely will) don't beat yourself up. Just brush off the dust, wipe the sugar off of your lips, and get back on the treadmill. God will meet you there.

YOU CAN MASTER NEW SKILLS

A wise man will hear and increase in learning,
and a man of understanding will acquire wise counsel.
PROVERBS 1:5 NASB

When we're young, we are filled with a sense of purpose and adventure. We're not afraid to try new things, especially new skills. Auditioning for a local play? Why not! Decorating cakes? Sure, we'll give it a try! Making our own baby food? Of course! These are fun skills to master. And who cares if we don't get it right? It's fun to try, right?

As we age, however, we often set those desires aside, unwilling to try new things. We get set in our ways and let the young people (or other women our own age, even) try new things. We watch as a friend picks up a new hobby and marvel as a coworker shows off photos of her latest quilt or crocheted shawl, but we're not really interested in acquiring new skills.

This is such a shame! God gave us incredible imaginations and intended for them to be used, not just in our youth, but all of our lives. There are so many untapped dreams, so many things we could be doing.

Margaret understood this better than most. As a young woman, she'd had a sense of adventure about her. Always ready to try new things, she acquired many artistic skills. But, as she aged, she let those desires wane. Until she went to her friend's house and saw a beautiful painting on the wall. One glimpse at the outdoor scene and she was

hooked. The colors. The fine "sweeps" of the brush. The nuances. She loved it all. And all of it made her want to pick up a brush.

She didn't, of course. What would her husband say? And her kids? So, she scribbled and scratched little designs in secret until she just couldn't take it anymore. A trip to the local craft store set her heart ablaze. She bought the necessary items, took them home, and got busy, painting. Sure, her husband was surprised, but he liked the idea. He liked it even more when people began to take interest. And her kids liked it so much that they began to ask for art pieces for their homes. Over a period of time, Margaret put together quite a collection. Best of all, the process of painting gave her quiet time to spend with the Lord. She could pray and paint at the same time.

What skill have you secretly longed to master but have been afraid to try? French cooking? Crocheting? Floral arranging? Why not sign up for a class? Or watch some online videos, then give it a shot. Interested in singing? Take some voice lessons or join a choir to further develop your skills. The point is, it's not too late. God can take your desires and put wings on them. You can master new skills and draw closer to your heavenly Father in the process.

YOU'VE GOT WORK TO DO

A sluggard's appetite is never filled,
but the desires of the diligent are fully satisfied.
PROVERBS 13:4 NIV

Lounging around. Hanging out in your PJs. Enjoying an old movie. Eating chocolates. These are all fun, relaxing things to do. But some women have a problem getting out of their "relaxed" mode and back into a "get the ball rolling again" state of mind. Let's face it: it's easy to get lethargic. But some folks let the word *sluggish* rule the day. Perhaps you've heard the old expression about how a body in motion tends to stay in motion and a body at rest tends to stay at rest. When you've been quiet and still, it's hard to get your momentum up.

Doris understood that. For months she worked herself to the bone. Hours of overtime. Working against the clock. Deadline after deadline. Finally, the holidays approached. She had a few weeks off to rest and enjoy herself. She put her on her pajamas and never wanted to take them off again. Sure, she knew the inevitable day was coming. She would have to get back in the saddle once again. But lounging around sounded a lot more fun. Nibbling on sweets. Watching movies. Resting on the sofa. And who needed to keep up with housework and dishes while on sabbatical? That could wait.

And wait it did, until her husband had had enough. While he appreciated her need for rest, he wasn't keen on the fact that the

house was flipped upside-down when he got home from work. He dove in and put things in order—without saying a word. He didn't have to. She got the point, and she got back to work. She moved slowly at first. Her body didn't seem to want to cooperate. Finally, she got her momentum back. Just in time to go back to work. Go figure.

Maybe you're like Doris. You love those seasons of rest and wish they didn't have to end. God instructs us in His Word to take a Sabbath break. In fact, He instituted the Sabbath for our good. But it's not meant to go on forever. Just remember, a "season" is just that: a season. It's not a "lounge on the sofa unbathed for three days" sort of thing. So, enjoy your downtime, but understand that God is probably preparing you for the road ahead, the work ahead. He's got big things planned for you and wants you to be in the best possible shape to enjoy it all.

It's not going to be easy, but you can do it. Stand up. Stretch. Take a walk around the house. Then, slowly but surely, get back to work, woman of purpose. You can do this.

YOU ARE BOUGHT WITH A PRICE

You were bought at a price. Therefore
honor God with your bodies.
1 CORINTHIANS 6:20 NIV

Imagine going to a fine art museum and seeing a valuable painting. It's about to be auctioned off and the opening bid is fifty thousand dollars. Wow! That's quite a work of art! It's worth far more than you might guess at first glance. As the crowd thins, you give it a closer look. Hmm. When you look at that so-called priceless piece, all you see is an ordinary painting. Maybe it's even a little odd looking. Abstract. Weird. You can't figure out why it's worth so much. It's certainly not something you would hang on your living room wall, even if someone paid you to do it!

What gives the painting its value is the artist. His name is imprinted on it. An ordinary painting is suddenly worth a fortune if van Gogh's name is on it. Rembrandt. Renoir. The very name adds value, regardless of the "look" of the painting. The outward package is irrelevant. The name means everything.

The same can be said of you, a priceless work of art. God's name is imprinted on your heart. You bear His name, His "stamp," if you will. That alone gives you immeasurable value. It makes you priceless, in fact. No one could bid high enough to purchase you because they couldn't pay the price. Only the Lord could do that, and He's already done it!

Think about that for a moment. You were bought with a price and

are more valuable than rubies or diamonds, more precious than any rare jewel, and more costly than any painting, no matter how famous the painter might be. The Master Artist took the time to craft you just as you are, a rare beauty.

How amazing to think that the ultimate Creator wove you together in your mother's womb. What a work of art! He already paid the price for you when He sent His Son to Calvary. You were worth so much to Jesus that He laid down His very life for you. Rarely would anyone pay a huge price (think of that art piece again) for something they loved . . .but it's almost impossible to think that someone (in this case, God Himself) would pay the price with His blood. How valuable you are to Him! Others might not see it, but He does! And He never forgets that you are His personal design, created in His image.

How are you viewing yourself today, woman of purpose? You are more valuable than any van Gogh. Keep that in mind the next time you glance in the mirror.

YOU ARE RADIANT

Arise, shine, for your light has come,
and the glory of the LORD has risen upon you.
ISAIAH 60:1 ESV

Have you ever seen those beautiful paintings that date back to the Renaissance era? Jesus is always portrayed with a heavenly glow around His head. For that matter, many of the saints and/or apostles were depicted the same way. The "heavenly glow" represented the radiant presence of God. These were the "set apart" ones, the ones who were sent to this earth to make a difference. And make a difference they did! If you ever had a question in your mind about which people were most holy, just look for the heavenly glow.

If you think about it, you have that same heavenly glow! It doesn't show up in photographs necessarily, but it draws people to you just the same. The Bible says that you are a reflection of Christ, and He's the most radiant of all. You shimmer and shine for all the world to see.

Sure there are days when you feel like someone's taken a giant eraser and wiped that glow away, but even on the worst of days you're still radiant. You let your light shine, and it makes a difference in the lives of those around you.

Just one word of warning as you go throughout your day, shining His light for all the world to see. Sometimes a light that's pointed right into someone's eyes can be blinding. Irritating. So as you are reflecting

His beautiful radiance, make sure you do so with love, in a way that isn't offensive or painful.

Deborah learned this lesson the hard way. She wanted to be a good witness to her friends, so she made a point of quoting scriptures and lecturing them whenever they strayed too far off the beaten path. Her intentions were good, but the outcome wasn't. People began to avoid her, calling her a Jesus freak or a religious nut. Instead of drawing people to the light, they ran in the opposite direction whenever they saw her coming. Why? Because they saw her as judgmental and unkind. Perhaps a more loving approach would've been better. She could've let her little light shine but kept it out of their eyes.

What about you? Does your light shine brightly, or has it flickered to a tiny wisp? Are you using it wisely? Ask the Lord to show you the best possible way to reflect His light so that you can share His love with others in need.

YOU ARE CAREFUL WHO YOU LISTEN TO

So be careful how you live. Don't live like fools,
but like those who are wise.
EPHESIANS 5:15 NLT

Oh be careful little eyes what you see. Oh be careful little ears what you hear." Likely, you grew up singing that little song. Women of purpose are exceptionally cautious when it comes to what they let their ears hear. Why? Because they know that actions surely follow, and sometimes those actions can have negative effects.

How does this play out in the real world? Often, we find ourselves sucked into conversations that we have no reason to be a part of. Before long, we're actually believing what we're hearing. Common sense tells us it's not true, but the emotion coming from the speaker's voice is convincing. So convincing, in fact, that it often propels us to do things we shouldn't. To make decisions we shouldn't.

Take Julie's story, for instance. She found herself in the center of a conversation about some drama that was supposedly going on at her church. None of it was her business, but she got drawn into the emotion of the story. The one telling the woeful tale had an obvious slant against the pastor. Julie didn't have any negative feelings toward the pastor. . . until she heard this story, which she believed, without even asking for a second opinion. She fussed and fumed over what she'd heard, finally convincing her husband that they probably needed to leave the church

and try to find a new church home. He was shocked, and responded with a line that really bugged her: "Let's pray about it and give it time."

Turned out, the story wasn't even true. Well, parts of it were, but it had definitely been skewed to favor someone else and not the pastor. Julie felt silly for getting sucked in so easily. From that point on she paid careful attention to who she listened to. . .and who she didn't.

Sometimes we just have to learn the hard way, don't we? Maybe you're caught up in the middle of some unexpected drama right now. Perhaps it's going on at work. Or within the family. Or at your church. Just be careful who you listen to. Remember, there are two sides to every story. Jesus wouldn't want you to judge based on someone else's hearsay. Go to the Lord, and ask for His opinion. His is the only one that really matters. His perspective is far more important than any gossip you might hear. And whatever you do, don't take action without knowing for sure that you're hearing pure truth. No slants. Nothing skewed.

Take another look at today's scripture. Be careful how you live. Be wise. This requires thoughtfulness. No impulsive moves. S-l-o-w down and think before you act, before you speak, before you make matters worse.

Oh be careful little ears what you hear. Just something to ponder, woman of purpose.

YOU'VE LEARNED TO LIVE A BALANCED LIFE

He replied, "You of little faith, why are you so afraid?"
Then he got up and rebuked the winds and the waves,
and it was completely calm.

MATTHEW 8:26 NIV

A woman of purpose is a woman of balance. She doesn't teeter too far to the right or the left. This is true in her health, her family life, her work. She's learned (sometimes the hard way) that walking the balance beam is tricky but possible.

Amy had a harder time than most with living in balance. She was like a pendulum, swinging back and forth. Dieting one day, binge eating the next. Organizing her home with a vengeance one day, letting things fall apart the next. Overcommitting herself at church one day, stopping all activities the next. She had a hard time learning how to find a healthy place in the middle. Amy finally learned a hard lesson, but one she never forgot—if you don't take on too much, you won't get too tired. If you don't adopt an extreme diet, you might actually be able to live with it. And so on. Problem was, she enjoyed the extremes. They offered excitement. Until she crashed, anyway.

Are you like Amy? Is your life filled with extremes? Are you an experience junkie? If so, chances are pretty good your pendulum is swinging back and forth in an unhealthy way. Maybe it's time to do a little inventory. Take a look at your activities, your choices, your daily

obligations, and make sure everything is in balance. If you're having to pull back over here to accommodate over there, a little tweaking might be in order. If you're having to give up sleep to get your work done, it's definitely time to prioritize.

Why do women of purpose need to live balanced lives? We need to stay healthy, for one thing. Unbalanced woman end up with all sorts of issues—poor eating habits high on the list. Lack of exercise. Stress. On and on it goes. And once your health is affected, your emotions are sure to follow.

So don't learn the hard way. Rest when you need to rest. Play when you need to play. Work when you need to work. Find a "sweet spot" with all three of those. And, above all, spend time with the Lord. Seek Him daily. Get in His Word for His perspective on your activities. Perhaps in doing so, He will speak to you regarding your busyness and give a strong sense of direction.

Balance, sweet friend. It's far more than walking a tightrope.

YOU CAN LEARN TO BE KINDER

So, as those who have been chosen of God, holy and beloved, put on a heart of compassion, kindness, humility, gentleness and patience.

COLOSSIANS 3:12 NASB

Unlike other traits, like joy for instance, kindness is a learned behavior. Even if it doesn't come naturally to you, it can be developed.

Don't believe it? Think of the poor children raised in a home with no kindness at all. Maybe they were shouted at day in and day out. They were never encouraged, never bragged about, never given pats on the back. And yet, miraculously, they grew up to be kind, loving adults. How did this happen? They learned kindness from outside sources—perhaps a kindhearted teacher or coach. Maybe a Sunday school teacher or neighbor. Someone intervened and made a huge difference in the life of those children, a difference that affected multiple generations.

We are called to be kind, and people are watching. They might even be learning from us. Of course, the ultimate teacher is Jesus Himself. He looked on others with such kindness and compassion in His heart. We learn in His Word how to treat others. It's not always easy to show kindness, but it's always the best choice.

Take Janetta's story, for instance. There was a certain boy on her son's softball team who made her a little crazy. He was a rough kid, from a not-so-great home (from what she could gather). The boy had

a lot of attitude and rarely treated the others well. Still, Janetta made up her mind to treat him kindly. The other parents on the team weren't so willing to go the distance with the kid, but Janetta never gave up. She spent quality time with him, asked about his school work, helped him with homework, and even managed to get her husband to help the boy with his pitching skills. Before long, the young man softened. Wonder of wonders. . .he got nicer! The other parents took note and responded. Before long, the entire dynamic of the team was different. This kindness eventually spilled over onto the boy's family, and multiple lives were changed, all because one woman decided to take the time to speak kindly.

Is there someone in your life like that young man in Janetta's story? We all have folks in our circle who are, well, difficult. They're just hard to be around. We have a hard time playing nice around them. Oh, but it's so worth it! Maybe you won't see the fruit of your kindness right away, but there will be a payoff sooner or later.

How can you show kindness? Have a pleasant disposition. Show concern. Instigate random acts of kindness when the person least suspects it. Pray and ask the Lord for His perspective. Most of all, learn to love the unlovable. It's worth it. *They* are worth it. After all, they are God's kids too.

YOU'VE GOT STYLE

Hospitable, a lover of good, self-controlled,
upright, holy, and disciplined.

TITUS 1:8 ESV

Marci was a woman with a lot of style. Her hair always looked great. She knew exactly how to pick out the right clothes, right down to the perfect accessories. Even her shoes matched her outfits. Friends always commented on how nice she looked. This "style" spilled over into her life as well. She was known for her kindness and for treating people with grace.

If people had wanted to investigate further, if they'd looked beyond the stylish clothes and the perfect hair, they might've noticed a woman with about sixty extra pounds. And the not-so-perfect teeth. But, no. They only saw the style, the grace, and the love. They saw the real her, and to them, she was gorgeous every time.

We all have a certain style about us, don't we? We have a particular manner of doing things. Our own mode, method, or "modus operandi." In a sense, we're our own "brand" (think of your favorite soda or chips here). People know us at a glance because of our style. Whether we're casual or fancy, quirky or fun, we're all styling. And like Marci, this spills over into our attitudes and behaviors.

So what's your style? When people look at you, what do they think? For some, they might take one look and say, "Wow, she looks like a

hoot! I'd like to get to know her!" For others they think, "Wow, she must really have money. Look at that jacket she's wearing." For others, the line might be, "Wow. Don't get close to that one. She looks scary!" This "first response" might seem a little judgmental on their part, but let's face it. . .we all pay attention to the other person's style, whether we acknowledge it or not.

What does style have to do with our spiritual walk? Quite a bit, if you think about it. We're not expected to put on a fashion show, so that's not the point. But we are representing Christ, so we don't want to turn up in public looking like a mess. Well, not all of the time, anyway. But more importantly, we want to be inviting. Our "style" shouldn't turn people away. It should draw them to us. When our demeanor is comfortable, inviting, people from every walk of life will find us approachable. And isn't that the point?

Jesus had His own style too. He wasn't handsome (according to the Bible), but people flocked to His side. This had nothing to do with His clothing, to be sure. It had everything to do with His compassion and love for others. His "style show" went far beyond the physical and served as an invitation to others to draw near, to sit at His feet and learn. To love and be loved.

Let's follow the example of Christ today, woman of purpose. Put on a style show like His, then watch as others are drawn to you.

YOU ARE A DAUGHTER OF THE KING

The King's daughter is all glorious within;
her clothing is interwoven with gold.

PSALM 45:13 NASB

Don't you just love today's scripture? What a beautiful image of you, the daughter of the King, adorned in golden clothing. Exquisite! And it's not out of character for God's girls to want to be princesses, to dress in fancy gowns, and live the life of a royal. We've been playing that role from the time we were very little. Think about it. Every little girl longs to dress up as a princess. The flowing gown. The crown. The jewels. Life in the castle. We want to skip from room to room in our Father's gorgeous house and greet our guests with flourish. Most of all we want to please our Daddy's heart. Nothing makes us happier than seeing the smile on the King's face as He looks adoringly at us.

Of course, we often grow up and completely forget about our childish desires. Dancing at the King's feet, to flitting from room to room in the castle. . .these are just silly memories. Gone are the days of seeing ourselves as lovely. Or graceful. Or royals. The cares and woes of life kick in and we totally abandon our little-girl dreams. But God hasn't forgotten. He's still the King of kings, and we're still His daughters!

Have you thought about how magnificent it is to be a daughter of the King? You're nobility! And how He adores us, His girls, His kids. Consider that in light of another scripture, Romans 8:14–17, which

tells us that we've been adopted by God. The Spirit makes us sons (and daughters) of the Most High God. Because of this, we cry, "Abba (Daddy) Father." We're heirs. Wow! Take that in. Heirs. We're set to inherit all that our Father has available for us.

Today, instead of running from the idea that you're royalty, why not spend some time in the presence of the King? Run to His courts. Settle in at His feet and ask Him what it means to be a daughter of the King. How can you best represent Him? How can you serve the Kingdom? How does a royal live?

Oh, daughter of God, you are precious in His sight. More precious than all of the jewels in the Kingdom. So don't run from your position any longer. Embrace it, and watch as the King lavishes His love on you.

Do not be overcome by evil,
but overcome evil with good.
ROMANS 12:21 NASB

If you've ever felt snowed under by life, then the word *overcome* should bring you hope. The Word of God promises that you—woman of purpose—are an overcomer. You're more than a survivor. . .you're a thriver.

So, what does it mean to overcome? If you break the word down, it means to "come over" a situation, to pass from one place to another. Think of the various hurdles and trials you face. They're like giant walls. You must get from one side to the complete opposite. To overcome means you "come over" the wall that divides the two. You make the leap, never to go back.

How do you cross from one side to the other? It's kind of like that game you used to play as a child: "Red Rover, Red Rover, let so-and-so come over." Remember what it was like? There you stood, hand-in-hand with your teammates. Then, in that moment, as your name was called, everyone looked to you to break free from the group and tear across the open field to the opposite side. There was something about the cheers from your team members that gave you the courage to let go and run, run, run, anticipating how you would break through the barrier. Then, as you crashed through, victory! So much energy, so much drive, from such a little girl!

The same is true in your faith walk. The book of Hebrews (chapter 11) refers to a great cloud of witnesses who are looking on as you run your race as a believer. Think of them as your Red Rover friends, standing hand-in-hand, encouraging you to break through. These witnesses are there for you, ready to teach you how to overcome. Whenever you need encouragement, just read their stories: Study Moses, who led his people to the Promised Land. Read about the life of Noah, who faced his fear and did what God commanded, though it made no sense at the time. Learn from Esther, who took a stand for her people and saved a nation. Still not convinced? Pause for a moment in the story of Jonah, who learned the hard way. Glean from young Timothy, who recognized God's gifts in his life. Discover the heart of an overcomer in young David, who faced the mighty Goliath with nothing but a slingshot and a few stones.

With the help of these very real people, you can learn how to get from one side of the obstacle to the other. You are an overcomer, indeed! Don't let anyone tell you otherwise.

YOU HAVE AN ADVOCATE

My dear children, I write this to you so that you will not sin.
But if anybody does sin, we have an advocate with
the Father—Jesus Christ, the Righteous One.
1 JOHN 2:1 NIV

If you've ever found yourself in a courtroom, you know the importance of having a representative, someone who can argue your case or speak on your behalf. The Bible says that God is our advocate. . .our representative.

Here are a few other words to define advocate: a supporter (someone willing to be there for you). A champion (someone who sees you as a winner, no matter what). A backer (someone who won't let you down; he/she agrees with you and takes a stand for you). A proponent (someone who argues for or supports something). A spokesperson (someone willing to speak up on your behalf). A crusader (someone willing to go to battle on your behalf).

Jesus is all of those things listed above, and He's intimately concerned about acting on your behalf. You don't even have to pay Him, like you would a good attorney. He represents you. . .for free. What an unbelievable blessing. He's pleading our case, not with words, but with His very life. When He sent His Son, Jesus, to die on the cross, He offered Himself in our place. He took the penalty for our sin. Talk about the ultimate middleman. Not that we deserved such grace, mind you. But we happily accept it.

Perhaps you're wondering why you need an advocate. A middleman is essential when we're unable to handle things on our own. This is particularly true as it relates to salvation. There's nothing we could do to earn our way to heaven, so we rely on Jesus' sacrifice. When it comes to day-to-day living, we always need to trust God to handle the things that we cannot. Whether it's work related, relational, or an issue at church, the Lord wants to be at the center of it all. So, if you're going through a situation you can't fix, go to your Advocate. If you're ill and don't know how to make yourself well, go straight to your Advocate. If you're in a relationship struggle and it appears people are going to be hurt, ask your Advocate to take control.

Jesus didn't just play the role of middleman on the cross, He still longs to be in the very middle of every difficulty you find yourself in. Don't be afraid to call on Him. He's ready, willing, and able to be your Advocate.

YOUR DREAMS CAN BE SUPERSIZED

And the LORD answered me: "Write the vision;
make it plain on tablets, so he may run who reads it.
For still the vision awaits its appointed time; it hastens
to the end—it will not lie. If it seems slow, wait for it;
it will surely come; it will not delay."

HABAKKUK 2:2–3 ESV

If you've ever been to a fast food restaurant, you know they always seem to ask the same question when you order a burger and fries and a drink: "Would you like to supersize that?" Most of the time we respond with a hearty "No!" knowing what the extra calories will do to our hips and thighs. But sometimes when life presents us with that same question, we should respond with a hearty, "Yes! Yes, I'd like to supersize that!"

This is especially true when it comes to our dreams. Sometimes we dream too small. Think about the disciples after Jesus died and was resurrected. Do you think they ever imagined the impact they would have on the world? Do you think they saw themselves traveling all over the place, spreading the Gospel like wildfire? At some point one or more of them had to cast the vision to do something larger than themselves.

That's what we have to do too. Don't believe it? Ask Madison. One day, in the middle of a worship service, she had what felt like a rather wacky "out there" idea. It involved opening up a Crisis Pregnancy Center for women. Having been through an unplanned pregnancy, she knew

what the women needed, but how in the world would she go about it? Still, she committed to pray about it. A few months later, a volunteer position opened up at a local pregnancy center. She took it. Two years later, the director moved on and the position opened up. Madison easily slipped into the role. Suddenly, the dream that had seemed so huge just a few years back was totally doable!

Dreaming big doesn't mean we're necessarily following after our own dreams or ideas. If we did that, we'd look like cats chasing their tails! No, to dream big means we pray, ask the Lord for His plans, then catch the vision! Once the vision's "caught," we jump onboard and run after it. Some of these dreams might seem too big to be realistic, but that's when we have to trust God.

You don't need a business plan. You need a prayer plan. You don't need someone to manage your dream; you need to submit it to the Lord. Once His will is revealed, get ready to roll up your sleeves, woman of purpose! What's ahead is much bigger—much more exciting—than any dream you've visited before. So, get ready. When God's in it, the plans are out of this world!

YOU ARE BEAUTIFUL

Do not let your adorning be external—the braiding of hair
and the putting on of gold jewelry, or the clothing you wear—
but let your adorning be the hidden person of the heart with
the imperishable beauty of a gentle and quiet spirit,
which in God's sight is very precious.

1 PETER 3:3–4 ESV

Most women have a hard time accepting the idea that they are beautiful. We tend to glance in the mirror and see every flaw. The wrinkles. The sagging skin. The blemishes. The extra pounds. What we don't see is the underlying beauty. In other words, we have a hard time with perspective. We don't see ourselves the way God sees us. If we could, we would recognize true beauty.

Still don't feel beautiful? You are! The Bible backs this up. We are the bride of Christ, and we're created in His image. He's a beautiful God. Do a search through the Bible for scriptures on the beauty of the Lord and you'll discover just how beautiful. It stands to reason that we're gorgeous in His sight, but we often don't want to admit it because it doesn't feel that way.

Because we can't see our inward beauty, we often rely on external things to "pretty things up." There's nothing wrong with wanting to look lovely on the outside, but if we skip the internal things, we're missing the boat. For example, what would be the point of putting on lovely eye

makeup and yet not paying attention to the things our eyes are drawn to? What would be the point of putting on lipstick and then using our mouth to speak ugly things to/about people? What would be the point of using concealer to cover blemishes on our skin but then deliberately wounding others with our actions?

Rebecca had a hard time figuring this out. She worked on her external appearance. . .a lot. Not that she needed to. She was already a natural beauty. People everywhere said so. But sometimes the inside didn't match the outside. Her words were harsh. Her attitude was cold. She wondered why people shied away whenever she would come around. Wasn't she drawing them in with her beauty? Obviously not. It took a while to figure it out, but she eventually got it and cleaned up her attitude so that the internal matched the external.

There's nothing we can do to the outward body to make the internal soul look pretty to others. Only our love, our kindness, our heartfelt compassion will beautify us from the inside out. And those things—like every good thing—come from the Father above.

YOU ARE A WOMAN OF LOVE

And so we know and rely on the love God has for us. God is
love. Whoever lives in love lives in God, and God in them.

1 JOHN 4:16 NIV

If someone were to ask you, "What is love, anyway?" how would you
respond? You might say it's all about feelings or attitudes. You might
say it's a strong attraction or affection. Someone would say that love
is benevolence, kindness, compassion. Caring for your fellow man. If
we look at the Word of God, however, we have to agree that love—real
love—is all about sacrifice. It's about giving of yourself for others.

Do you consider yourself a woman of love? If you follow Jesus Christ,
if you spend time in His Word, then love surely radiates from every pore.
Okay, maybe you don't always feel like expressing it (especially on the
tough days), but God will move through you if you ask Him to. This is
possible, even when your feelings contradict. In fact, that's one way to
know for sure that God is on the move, if He loves through you when
you just aren't feeling it.

The ultimate example of real love is Jesus Christ, God's Son. If
you were to do a search in the Bible using the words "Jesus" along
with "love," you would come up with hundreds of scriptures. What a
wonderful example we have in our Savior! Every act of service, every
time He healed a sick or lame person, every time He fed a hungry crowd,
Jesus was teaching us how to love. Whenever He stilled the storm and

taught His disciples how to fish, He was really showing His love for the people He cared about. We need to learn to care just as deeply, to sacrifice just as intensely.

Today, make love your primary focus. If you happen to rub up against people who are tough to love, ask the Lord to show you how to love them as He loves you. He will, you know. He will give you His vision for that person. You will see them through a "Christ-lens," and what you see might just shock you. Behind the bitterness, the sour expression, the tough facade is a child of the King who needs someone to step up and love them, even when they don't deserve it.

Do you have it in you to love the unlovable? If so, then don't hesitate. Ask the Lord to show you one person per day that you can love in an extraordinary way. It might not be easy, but for a woman of purpose it's definitely doable.

YOU MAKE A DIFFERENCE

For God did not send his Son into the world to condemn
the world, but to save the world through him.

JOHN 3:17 NIV

Mary watched as an artist worked on a new painting. For the first few
minutes she couldn't make any sense of his color choices and couldn't quite
figure out where he was heading with the project. Then as he added just
a hint of brown to the top of the canvas, she realized. . .he was painting
a man's face. After that, everything else made sense. It all came into
perspective. Sometimes life is like that. We can't make any sense out of
where things are heading. We wonder if the road is moving forward at all.

There are so many people in this world who feel stuck. They can't
seem to get past where they are right here, right now. Life's circumstances
have them frozen in place. These people are all around us. The woman
at the grocery store. The child on the bicycle. The man in the business
suit. They might look perfectly normal on the outside, but on the inside
many feel disillusioned, like a painting with no color. Their lives aren't
turning out the way they'd hoped. Hopelessness has set in.

What does this have to do with being a difference maker? Everything.
You can be that splash of color that brings sense to a senseless picture.
You can give a word of encouragement to set them free. You can offer
hope when they're feeling hopeless.

Here's an example: Mary had a friend, a single mother with six

children. They lived in abject poverty and didn't know from day to day where their food would come from. Mary intervened and got her church's food pantry involved. Before long, the mother and children were in a much better place, and not just their bellies. They soon joined the church, gave their hearts to the Lord, and got involved in the various ministries. One of the daughters went on to serve on the worship team, eventually leading worship. All because one person took the time to share some food with them. That little splash of color from Mary brought the whole picture into focus for the mother and six children.

Difference makers aren't looking after their own happiness. They strive to be useful. They have genuine compassion for others. They put action to their words and produce fruit in their lives. Instead of saying, "I wonder how I can get more out of this day," they say, "I wonder how I can make this day better for someone else." Then they pray that God will send people in their path who need a special touch.

Who are you going to touch today? What splashes of color will you add to a friend (or stranger's) life? Open yourself up to the possibilities, then watch as God opens a door for you to make a difference—possibly a life-changing difference—when you least expect it.

YOU'VE GOT TO CELEBRATE GOD'S PLANS

"For I know the plans I have for you," says the LORD.
"They are plans for good and not for disaster,
to give you a future and a hope."
JEREMIAH 29:11 NLT

Have you ever noticed that God's plans don't always match up with our own? We're so good at setting things in motion—and many of us are equally as good at carrying through—but what happens when we get ahead of God? Have you ever done that?

Misty did. She often came up with terrific God-like ideas. They were very spiritual, in fact. Some of them included teaching a Bible study. Working with the homeless. Starting a ministry for single moms. Opening her home to teens in crisis. Working at a shelter. On and on it went, and all of it beneficial to the Kingdom of God. Lives were changed. People were blessed.

Good stuff, right? Only, the timing wasn't always right. And her husband wasn't always fully onboard. Sometimes she did these things, not because she'd prayed about them and had God's stamp of approval, but because it "seemed" like the right thing to do.

So let's break that down, woman of purpose. Likely, you're just as driven as Misty. Have you ever gotten the cart ahead of the horse? Ever stepped out on the road without God's say-so? If so, then you know that "oops!" feeling that can come along with it.

Bathing decisions in prayer is key, especially when you're loaded with zeal and drive. And when you sense the call of God on your life to make a difference in the world, you've got to be even more careful! You're likely to jump onboard every project, simply because you see the good in it.

And there is good in it! So much good, in fact, that someone else might get some benefit out of heading it up. Did you ever think about that? If you step back, someone else might get a chance to be blessed by taking on the project. Sure, you won't have the satisfaction of saying, "I did that!" but do you really need to?

Prayer. Slow decisions. Accountability partners. These are all good things for women of purpose. They keep us in balance. Ultimately, being in balance frees us up to do the things that God has truly called us to do, the things that we can excel at. So, take your time. Don't jump in headfirst. Seek God first and then take a deep breath. . .and wait. His plans for your life are perfect. Yours? Not so much.

YOUR HOME IS A SAFE HAVEN

The wise woman builds her house,
but with her own hands the foolish one tears hers down.
PROVERBS 14:1 NIV

When you think of the word *home*, what comes to mind? Besides thinking about the particular house or apartment you might live in, the word conjures up feelings of family, warmth, and safety. A refuge from the storm. In your home you're comfortable. You can let your hair down, kick your shoes off, cuddle up on the sofa with the dog next to you. You can share stories about the day and decompress without fear of judgment. Home is the place where people come when they're hurting, a place where tears are wiped away and broken hearts are mended.

As a woman of purpose, you have an obligation to make your home a place of safety, not just for your sake, but for your family and friends as well. This means you have to be careful what you allow into your home. You should guard what comes through your television and even the music that plays in your house. It might also mean you have to be discriminating when it comes to *who* you allow in your home. Think of yourself as a guardian standing at the door. A certain level of discernment is called for. Why do you have to be so careful? Because, as a safe haven, your home is a shelter. A sanctuary, if you will. If you're not careful, you open your home up to things—and people—who won't care about this as much as you do.

Candace learned this the hard way. She allowed her teenaged daughter to bring friends into the house when she was at work. Because Candace wasn't there to supervise, things went south in a hurry. Though they all went to the same church, these so-called "friends" weren't all they presented themselves to be. Before long, the unthinkable happened. Alcohol. Drugs. Police. Candace's daughter ended up in a courtroom facing a judge, along with a host of other teens. Who took the hardest hit—both from the judge and the other parents? Candace.

Maybe you've experienced something similar in your home. Or maybe you're overly cautious so that you never go down that road. Regardless, you've got to keep your spiritual eyes open wide. When you have some free time, pray over your house. Go from room to room, door to door, and pray over every part. Pray for God's peace to be upon everyone who enters and for those who dwell in the house to live in safety. Then, take inventory of the things you've allowed in your home. Start fresh by removing anything that doesn't line up with the Word of God. With a plan in place, your home can be a safe haven for all who enter.

YOU LOVE GOD'S WORD

For the word of God is alive and active.
Sharper than any double-edged sword,
it penetrates even to dividing soul and spirit,
joints and marrow; it judges the thoughts
and attitudes of the heart.

HEBREWS 4:12 NIV

If you're an avid reader, a true book lover, you find it hard to put a good story down. You'll try to get by with reading "just a chapter" before bed but find yourself turning the page to the next chapter, and then the next. The stories captivate you, draw you in.

The Bible is loaded with life-changing stories that will keep you on the edge of your seat. True swashbuckling heroes fighting formidable foes. Damsels in distress. Men of valor. Women of courage. The stories weave in and out in a lovely array, drawing you in and speaking a resounding message of faith. Best of all, they serve as an example of fortitude, tenacity, and pressure under fire. In short, they are better than any fictional story you will ever read because these heroes really existed. They walked on this earth and faced many of the same challenges that you face.

Have you paused to think that through? Moses was very real. So was Abraham. And Elijah. And David. And Deborah. All of the great difference makers were real men and women who passionately loved

the Lord and lived to serve Him. Their stories are more than just tales of good and evil; they're real pictures of people—like you—who faced battles head-on and won.

Do you ever wonder if these great men and women realized their stories would be passed down? Did they have any concept that, thousands of years later, people would glean from their life lessons? It's fun to think about how the story of God's people has carried on, well past Bible times into the present. And you're part of that story. If the great writers of old were still penning stories of faith, yours would slide right in alongside the others. People could read it hundreds or even thousands of years from now.

When you see the Bible in perspective, as more than just a storybook . . .when you read about the life and ministry of Jesus and His journey to the cross. . .you can't help but stand in awe that this marvelous Word has stood the test of time and is ours, even today. It is, by far, the most valuable book you will ever read, loaded with answers for every question, examples for every life challenge, and wisdom for every decision. No wonder you love it so much, woman of purpose! In it, you find all you will ever need!

Well, what are you waiting for? Go grab that Bible and dive in! There are heroes of the faith just waiting for you to share their stories.

Anything I wanted, I would take. I denied myself
no pleasure. I even found great pleasure in
hard work, a reward for all my labors.
ECCLESIASTES 2:10 NLT

Think about the ants, all lined up in a row, building their mound. On and on they march, in perfect unison until the job is done. You rarely see one step out of line or breaking rank. No, they all stick together because they've learned the secret: their work matters. And when they all work together, they can accomplish something grand.

The body of Christ is made up of all sorts of people with all sorts of gifts and abilities. Maybe you think, in the grand scheme of things, that your contribution is small in comparison to others. You see the übertalented and shrug, saying, "Well, I'll never be able to sing like her" or "I can't possibly teach a Bible study like that woman."

Julia felt that way. . .for a while, anyway. She helped out at her church on Sunday mornings making coffee and preparing trays of donuts. No big deal, right? Didn't seem like much to her. She got to know a couple of the other ladies in the kitchen, including Diana, who was going through a rough patch in her marriage. Julia listened to Diana's struggles and prayed for her. Most of all, she provided a warm hug and a comforting smile, along with words of encouragement. Still, Julia didn't consider any of this "Kingdom work."

Oh, but it was! Like those diligent ants, Julia was making a difference. She was part of something bigger than herself. Handing out coffee and donuts was part of the plan, yes, but the bigger plan was her growing relationships with the ladies she worked with. Bonding. Growing together. Overcoming obstacles.

Maybe you're like Julia. You don't consider your "contribution" to the body of Christ to be significant. Maybe working in the nursery seems like small potatoes compared to leading worship or heading up the women's ministry. It's not small potatoes to those babies or their mamas. Maybe volunteering in the church office one day a week doesn't even feel like work at all. You have such a good time visiting with those who come and go. And folding church bulletins? It's pure delight when you share the job with a friend.

Your work matters. And when we all work together, like those ants, we create a thing of beauty, something much larger than ourselves. Every worker is equally important to the whole. So think about that the next time you're tempted to quit. What you do makes a huge difference to the body of Christ.

YOU ARE CONSTANT IN PRAYER

Be joyful in hope, patient in affliction, faithful in prayer.

ROMANS 12:12 NIV

At the beginning of the New Year, Julie had every intention of reading her Bible every day and praying at a specific time. She did well for the first week or so but then started slipping. Having a set time to read and pray didn't always work out for her, and she often ended up feeling guilty if she missed out.

Maybe you're like Julie. You've tried to get in the routine of reading and praying at the same time every day. For many women, this works great. Others have a harder time sticking to a set schedule. While it's a great idea to try to read a certain number of chapters a day or pray for a set length of time, what's really important here is maintaining a desire to meet with the Lord and spend time with Him. It's your heart He's after, not a certain number of minutes.

Imagine you had a really good friend, one you talked with every day. She was your "go to" person whenever you had a problem. The two of you shared pretty much everything. Then, one day, she married and moved away to another state. You still "saw" each other on social media and occasionally spoke by phone, but she was now happily married and not as free to talk all the time. You would miss her, right? Most of all, you would miss the intimate conversations and the comfort you felt just knowing you had someone you could run to.

Now think about that in light of prayer. God is the ultimate One we can go to when we're needing someone to listen. Those intimate conversations you're lacking with your friend? The Lord is hoping you'll want to share them with Him. That's what prayer is. . .a sweet one-on-one conversation with someone you love. And who loves you more than the One who created you?

So stop thinking about prayer as a "have to" thing. It's not a drudgery. It's a sweet conversation in passing. It's a lengthy pour-out-your-heart episode. It's a quick, rushed "Please Lord, protect me!" It's a quiet "Thank You for your blessings, Father," followed by a list of things you're most grateful for. It's a tearful "I don't get it, Lord" when things are falling apart and a "Praise the Lord! Hallelujah!" when all is going well.

In short, prayer is a day-in-and-day-out conversation with God. He doesn't care if you meet with Him at 6:00 a.m. or noon. What matters to Him is the desire to come to Him with all of your cares, concerns, joys, and sorrows. He will meet you there and wipe away every tear.

YOU SPEAK LIFE

The Spirit alone gives eternal life. Human effort
accomplishes nothing. And the very words I
have spoken to you are spirit and life.

JOHN 6:63 NLT

Words have power. How often we forget this. We get caught up in the moment and say things like, "I'm no good at this" or "I've never been pretty." The more we speak these negative things, the more likely we are to believe them.

God wants our words to be positive, to ring true with life and energy that will propel us and encourage us. Our words also need to be positive when we're speaking to others. Sometimes this requires thinking carefully before we say anything.

Susan had a tendency to speak first and repent later, especially when it came to her friends. She freely offered advice, even when they didn't seek it. When her best friend started dating a guy that Susan wasn't crazy about, she spoke up. Loudly. And when another friend wore a new dress to a party that Susan didn't care for, she made it known in a not-so-flattering sort of way. Her words didn't exactly leave everyone feeling warm and fuzzy. In fact, she usually just got people riled up. Susan didn't particularly care about hurting feelings; she just spoke her mind. She didn't even mince words when cutting herself down. Many times she would spout off things like, "Oh, I know I'm fat. Who cares?" If she

cared, no one knew it. She didn't even flinch as the words were spoken.

A lot of people do that. They just open their mouths and insert their foot. Instead of apologizing, half the time they don't even realize they've hurt feelings. Maybe you've been on the receiving end. Or maybe, just maybe, you're more prone to dish it out.

Where do you fit in this scenario? Do you think before you speak or do you just let it all hang out? Do you worry about hurting feelings or do you have an "I don't care" attitude? You should care. Very much, in fact! You should care because the Lord cares. It breaks His heart when He sees us speak negatively. The tongue is a powerful weapon, which can be used for great good (to build up) or for bad (to tear down). If it's true that your tongue actually has the power of life and death in it, wouldn't you want to see it used to bring life to those around you?

Think of the words that were spoken over you as a child, both the positive and the negative ones. They took root. They affected you (sometimes into your adulthood). That's how powerful words are. They have sticking power. So choose them carefully. They're going to stick with people for a very long time.

YOU BELIEVE IN MIRACLES

I ask you again, does God give you the Holy Spirit
and work miracles among you because you obey
the law? Of course not! It is because you believe
the message you heard about Christ.

GALATIANS 3:5 NLT

Miranda stood at the beside of her cousin, praying, praying, praying.
Lilly had been in a coma for three days, and her prognosis wasn't good.
Doctors weren't sure she would make it. Miranda refused to give up.
She stormed heaven's gates, pleading with the Almighty to spare her
cousin's life. Even when others told her to give up, she simply couldn't.

About two weeks later, Lilly showed signs of improvement. It took
time, but she eventually awoke from the coma. The journey was long
and arduous, but Miranda never gave up. She prayed diligently and
believed with her whole heart that God would completely restore her
cousin. Lilly continued to improve and eventually left the hospital and
returned to a normal life, free of any indicators that she had almost
lost the battle.

Sometime later, Miranda prayed for her father, who was diagnosed
with cancer. This time, in spite of her firm belief in miracles, he did not
survive. He passed away just two years after Lilly's miraculous recovery.
Miranda was devastated for a short season, but eventually came to
grips with the fact that God had, in His own way, answered her prayers

for a miracle. In taking her dad home to heaven, the Lord had granted the ultimate healing, one where her father would never experience any more pain. She didn't understand it but reconciled herself to the fact that God was sovereign and His will was perfect. In other words, she didn't need to have the "why" question answered. Not in this life, anyway. Maybe one day she would get answers, but in the meantime she would continue to trust God and believe for big things.

We don't know how situations will end, but we know that we serve a miracle-working God. And while some believe that miracles ended when the last apostle died, the Bible simply doesn't back that up. According to the Word of God, miracles are still happening today, all around us. And a woman of purpose believes wholeheartedly in God's ability to move miraculously in her life and in the lives of people around her. No, things don't always end the way we hope and pray. But that doesn't stop us from praying. If we're diligent in prayer, we will witness many, many miracles in our lifetime—people healed from illnesses, loved ones walking away from catastrophic car accidents, and much more.

What are you believing God for today? Cling tight to your faith, even if it seems impossible. This might just be the day the Lord surprises you with a miracle of biblical proportions.

YOUR BEST DAYS ARE AHEAD

There are many who say, "Who will show us some good?
Lift up the light of your face upon us, O LORD!"

PSALM 4:6 ESV

Have you ever looked back on your life and thought, *Man, I had it so good when I was younger!* Many of us wish we could go back in time and relive some of the "good old days." Oh, the stories we could tell about the adventures we used to have when we were young.

Here's something fun to think about, woman of purpose: Your best days are actually ahead of you, not behind you! It's true! The road ahead is loaded with adventures. For some, that's great news. Maybe your past wasn't so great and you're thrilled with the idea that what's in front of you will be better.

Some have a hard time believing it though. Take Donna, for instance. Well into her seventies, she faced life as a widow. She hadn't planned to outlive her spouse, but that's exactly what happened. George passed away suddenly after forty wonderful years of marriage. This left a void in Donna's heart—and her home. She didn't believe for a minute that her best years were ahead of her. She had her memories and they kept her company. No point in dreaming about the future. She wouldn't be around long enough to enjoy it anyway. With George gone, what did it matter?

Only, she *was* around for years to come. Donna enjoyed exceptionally good health. She eventually gave in to the pleading of a daughter and

joined a quilting group at her church. Before long, she was the queen bee of the group, leading the pack in "Round Robins" and quilting retreats. Best of all, she was able to create a memory quilt to commemorate her husband's life. Looking at that quilt brought comfort, not just to Donna, but to her daughter and grandchildren as well.

Something wonderful happened as Donna dove into her work. A renewed zeal rose up in Donna's heart whenever she reached for the quilt squares. More than just "something to do," the quilts brought her great joy. Placing the stitches was therapeutic. . .healing.

Are you like Donna? Have you decided that your best years are behind you? Don't give up! You are a woman of purpose, no matter your age or situation. If only you could see what the Lord has planned for you on the road ahead. You'd be so excited! There are adventures a'plenty, and you've got to have the excitement to face them. So, brace yourself. Get ready. Don't settle into that easy chair just yet, sweet sister! The road ahead is waiting.

YOUR JOB ISN'T FINISHED

Keep his decrees and commands, which I am giving
you today, so that it may go well with you and your
children after you and that you may live long in the
land the LORD your God gives you for all time.

DEUTERONOMY 4:40 NIV

Many women look forward to their retirement years so that they can rest from their labors. There's nothing wrong with that. But long after your day job ends, long after the kids are grown and your hair is turning gray, the "work" of the Lord continues.

It's fun to think about how you can spend your time making a difference in the lives of others as the years go by. Maybe you'll volunteer at a homeless shelter. Perhaps you'll go on missions trips or help build homes at Habitat for Humanity. Maybe you'll work at your church's food pantry or help in the children's ministry. The options are endless!

There's no reason to wait until the Golden Years to dive in, either! There's so much work to do. There are homeless people who need blankets, children who need hugs, pastors who need encouragement. There are families in need of food, friends in need of care, and foster children in need of a warm home. This is a great big world with great big needs.

Starting to get the picture? There are so many people to be reached, so many souls to be won, so many fellow believers in need of love. . .

and you have the capability of touching many of them. Ask the Lord to show you how you can do His work. When you're tuned in to God's adventurous plan for your life, it won't feel like work. It will feel like bliss. That's really the only word to describe the feeling you'll have when you're in the flow of what the Holy Spirit is doing.

Oh, what an amazing thing, to be used by God to touch others. Really, is there any greater joy? We've been given this precious time on planet earth—just a blink of an eye, really—to make a huge difference. What role will you play? How many people will you meet in heaven whose lives were somehow impacted by yours here on earth?

You are a blessing to the body of Christ. You are a woman of purpose. You are focused on God, on others, and on your own spiritual growth. More than anything, you are a woman who points others to new life, new hope. And you will go on doing that for every wondrous moment of your life. May God richly bless you as you continue to work for Him.

SCRIPTURE INDEX

OLD TESTAMENT

New Testament